Apache Spark
100 Interview Questions

X.Y. Wang

Contents

4 Advanced 71

5 Expert   105

Chapter 1

Preface

In the ever-evolving landscape of big data, Apache Spark has emerged as a luminary, casting its light on the vast possibilities of distributed data processing. Its rapid ascent in the tech world is not just a testament to its scalability and speed, but also to its flexibility in handling diverse data workloads, from batch processing to real-time analytics, from machine learning to graph processing. As organizations worldwide harness the power of big data, Spark has become an indispensable tool in their arsenal, driving transformative insights and innovations.

"Apache Sparks: 100 Interview Questions" is not just a book—it's a journey. A journey that takes you from the foundational concepts of Spark to its intricate internals, from its broad applications to the nuances of its deployment in varied environments. Whether you're a budding data engineer seeking to make a mark in the Spark ecosystem, a seasoned data scientist aiming to harness Spark's capabilities, or a hiring manager looking to gauge the depth of a candidate's Spark expertise, this book is your compass.

The questions contained within these pages have been meticulously curated to cover a broad spectrum of Spark's universe. They re-

flect the challenges faced in real-world scenarios, the depth of understanding required to optimize Spark applications, and the breadth of
knowledge needed to innovate. They are categorized by difficulty levels, ensuring that readers can navigate through them based on their
familiarity and experience with Spark.

But why focus on interview questions? Interviews are more than just
a gateway to job opportunities. They are a reflection of industry
needs, a snapshot of current trends, and a measure of the depth and
breadth of knowledge required in the field. By framing this book
around interview questions, we aim to provide readers with a focused
and practical understanding of Spark, aligned with what the industry
seeks.

As you delve into this book, you'll find questions that challenge your
understanding, provoke your curiosity, and inspire deeper exploration.
Each question is an opportunity to learn, to grow, and to prepare.
Whether you're on either side of the interview table, or simply a
curious mind seeking to master Spark, "Apache Sparks: 100 Interview
Questions" promises to be an invaluable resource.

Welcome to the world of Apache Spark. Let's ignite the journey of
discovery together.

Chapter 2

Basic

2.1 What is Apache Spark?

Apache Spark is an open-source, distributed computing system used for big data processing and analytics. It provides an interface for programming entire clusters with parallelism and fault-tolerance. It was originally developed at the University of California, Berkeley's AMPLab, and later donated to the Apache Software Foundation in 2013.

Apache Spark can process data from a variety of data repositories, including Hadoop Distributed File System (HDFS), NoSQL databases and relational data stores, such as Apache Hadoop. It supports a wide range of computational tasks, from conducting simple data transformations and filters to more complex machine learning and graph processing algorithms.

A key feature of Spark is its in-memory computing capabilities. It stores data in the Random Access Memory (RAM) of the computing resource, which helps to speed up iterative algorithms or interactive data mining tasks.

The core of the Spark engine operates on Resilient Distributed Datasets (RDDs), an abstraction of a distributed collection of items. RDDs offer two types of operations: transformations, which create a new dataset from an existing one, and actions, which return a value to the driver program after running a computation on the dataset.

Here's an example of creating a simple Spark RDD from a Python list and performing a map (transform) and a reduce (action) operation:

```
from pyspark import SparkConf, SparkContext

# Create a spark configuration with 20 threads
conf = (SparkConf()
    .setMaster("local[20]")
    .setAppName("My app")
    .set("spark.executor.memory", "1g"))

# create a spark context object
sc = SparkContext(conf=conf)

# Create a simple RDD
rdd = sc.parallelize(range(1,100))

# Define a function to apply to each element in the RDD
def add_one(x):
    return x + 1

# Use map to apply the function to each element in the RDD
rdd2 = rdd.map(add_one)

# Add up the elements in the RDD
sum = rdd2.reduce(lambda a, b: a + b)
```

In addition to Python, Spark also supports programming in Java, Scala, and R, and includes libraries for SQL (Spark SQL), Machine Learning (MLlib), Graph computation (GraphX), and stream processing (Spark Streaming).

2.2 How does Spark differ from Hadoop?

Apache Spark and Hadoop are both big data frameworks, but they differ mainly in their approach to processing big data.

1. **Processing Speed**: Spark is known for its speed, it can process data up to 100 times faster in memory and 10 times faster on disk

than Hadoop. This is mainly because Spark performs computations in memory during the later stages of data processing, which leads to less time spent on reading and writing data to disk.

For example, in machine learning tasks, where iterative computations are needed, Spark can keep the intermediary results in memory (caching), while Hadoop MapReduce has to write intermediary results to disk which makes it slower.

2. **Ease of Use**: Spark offers high-level APIs that make it both easy to write and to read the program. It supports APIs in languages like Java, Scala, Python, and R. Additionally, Spark provides built-in APIs for SQL, machine learning, graph processing (GraphX), and stream processing (Spark Streaming).

For example, here is how you can count the number of lines containing 'Spark' in a text file using Python in Spark:

```
textFile = spark.textFile("hdfs://...")
linesWithSpark = textFile.filter(lambda line: "Spark" in line)
numSpark = linesWithSpark.count()
```

The same task would require considerably more code in Hadoop MapReduce.

3. **Data Processing**: Hadoop uses MapReduce to process data, which is a batch-processing system. On the other hand, Spark not only supports batch processing but also interactive queries and streaming.

4. **Fault Tolerance**: Both Hadoop and Spark are fault-tolerant, but they achieve this in different ways. Hadoop writes data to disk after each map and reduce operation, which gives it high fault tolerance. Spark, on the other hand, uses the resilient distributed dataset (RDD) abstraction, which requires less space and makes it fault-tolerant. An RDD is an immutable distributed collection of objects, which can be processed in parallel.

5. **Data Storage**: Hadoop uses HDFS (Hadoop Distributed File System) for storage, while Spark doesn't have its own storage system

and it can use data stored in HDFS, Cassandra, AWS S3, and other data storage systems.

In sum, while Hadoop MapReduce shines in cases where data is too big to fit into the memory, Spark works better when faster processing speeds are required.

2.3   What are the main features of Apache Spark?

Apache Spark is a unified computing engine and a set of libraries for parallel data processing on computer clusters. Some of its main features include:

1. **Ease of Use**: Spark offers high-level APIs in Java, Scala, Python, and R, and an interactive shell/scala/java python for Scala and Python, respectively. This facilitates application development and enables a seamless developer experience.

2. **Speed**: Spark is known for high processing speed. Spark's in-memory computing capabilities make it much faster than other big data technologies such as Hadoop. This is especially advantageous for machine learning applications where iterative algorithms can greatly benefit from the caching ability of Spark.

3. **Multiple Format Support**: Spark supports various data sources such as Hive, Avro, Parquet, ORC, JSON, and JDBC. It can access diverse data sources including HDFS, Alluxio, Apache Cassandra, Apache HBase, and Amazon S3.

4. **Generality**: Spark combines SQL, streaming, and complex analytics in the same application. It includes libraries such as Spark-SQL, Spark Streaming, MLib (for Machine Learning), and GraphX (for Graph computation), enabling a broad range of analyses.

5. **In-memory computing**: Spark provides an in-memory com-

puting feature to increase the speed of data processing tasks.

6. **Fault Tolerance**: Spark offers inbuilt fault tolerance feature with the help of RDDs (Resilient Distributed Datasets). Spark's RDDs function as a working set for distributed programs offering a recoverable and distributed shared memory.

7. **Real-time computation**: With Spark Streaming, Spark can process real-time data and deliver near-instant analytics.

8. **Scalability**: Spark can manage to run clusters with thousands of nodes.

9. **Lazy Evaluation**: Apache Spark delays its evaluation till it is absolutely necessary. This is one of the key factors contributing to its speed.

Example of using its features in Python:

```python
from pyspark import SparkContext, SparkConf

#Step 1: Initialize SparkContext
conf = SparkConf().setAppName("AppName").setMaster("local")
sc = SparkContext(conf=conf)

#Step 2: Load data into RDD
data = [1, 2, 3, 4, 5]
distData = sc.parallelize(data)

#Step 3: Transform data using map and reduce
result = distData.map(lambda x: x * x).reduce(lambda x, y: x + y)

print(result) # Prints 55, as per the computations

#Step 4: Shutdown SparkContext to free up resources
sc.stop()
```

This simple example showcases Spark's basic operations like initializing a SparkContext, loading data into RDDs (Resilient Distributed Datasets), performing transformations using Spark's 'map' and 'reduce' functions, and shutting down the SparkContext.

2.4   What is RDD (Resilient Distributed Dataset)?

Resilient Distributed Datasets (RDD) is a fundamental data structure of Apache Spark. It's an immutable distributed collection of objects that can perform parallel operations. RDDs are designed to handle failures and are split into multiple partitions, which may be stored on different nodes within the cluster.

Here are some key features of RDD.

1. **Immutability:** Once the data is loaded into an RDD, it cannot be changed.

2. **Resilience:** If any partition of an RDD is lost, it can be re-computed using transformations.

3. **Distributed Nature:** RDD easily gets distributed across multiple nodes and operates on top of it.

4. **Lazy Evaluation:** Transformations are not executed instantly. They are recorded & executed when action is triggered, optimizing the overall data processing plan.

Creating an RDD in Python

```
from pyspark import SparkConf, SparkContext

# Spark Configuration
conf = SparkConf().setMaster("local").setAppName("My␣App")

# SparkContext Object
sc = SparkContext(conf = conf)

# creating an RDD
rdd = sc.parallelize(range(10)) # rdd: [0, 1, 2, 3, 4, 5, 6, 7, 8, 9]
```

In the code above, 'parallelize()' is a method to create an RDD from existing iterable objects in the driver program.

RDD supports two types of operations:

1. **Transformations:** These are operations on RDDs that yield another RDD, for example, map, filter, and reduce.

2. **Actions:** These are operations that yield values after running computations on RDDs, for example, count, collect, first, and take.

Remember, all transformations in Spark are lazy, they do not result in computed value. Instead, they are methods that are allow Apache Spark to operate on given RDDs.

For example, Running a 'map()' transformation will return a new RDD, but it does not immediately perform the transformation.

2.5 Name the languages supported by Apache Spark.

Apache Spark supports four main programming languages:

1) Scala: Spark is written in Scala and, as such, Scala is able to achieve very high performance with Spark. It is also the most used language with Spark.

2) Python: Because of the broad and deep support in data analytics, rich set of libraries and ease of use, and data science tools, Python is popular among data scientists. Spark provides PySpark API that supports Python with Spark.

3) Java: Java is broadly used in industry. Spark provides Spark Java API that allows Java developers to write Spark code using Java.

4) R: Sparklyr and SparkR API allow R users to leverage Spark capabilities. R is particularly popular among statisticians and is gaining popularity in data science.

2.6 What is Spark Streaming?

Apache Spark Streaming is an extension of the core Spark API that enables scalable, high-throughput, fault-tolerant stream processing of live data streams.

Data can be ingested from many sources like Kafka, Flume, Kinesis, or TCP sockets, and can be processed using complex algorithms expressed with high-level functions like 'map', 'reduce', 'join', and 'window'. Processing can happen in near real-time, depending on how fast the data is ingested and can be processed.

Spark Streaming takes in live streams of data, divides it into small batches and then processes these small batches in the Spark engine. The Spark Streaming APIs closely match those of the core Spark APIs, making it easy for developers to work with.

Here is an example of a Spark Streaming application in Scala that counts the words in text data received from a data server listening on a TCP socket:

```
import org.apache.spark._
import org.apache.spark.streaming._
import org.apache.spark.streaming.StreamingContext._

// Create a local StreamingContext with two working thread and batch interval
    of 1 second.
val conf = new SparkConf().setMaster("local[2]").setAppName("NetworkWordCount"
    )
val ssc = new StreamingContext(conf, Seconds(1))

// Create a DStream that will connect to hostname:port, like localhost:9999
val lines = ssc.socketTextStream("localhost", 9999)

// Split each line into words
val words = lines.flatMap(_.split(" "))

// Count each word in each batch
val pairs = words.map(word => (word, 1))
val wordCounts = pairs.reduceByKey(_ + _)

// Print the first ten elements of each RDD generated in this DStream to the
    console
wordCounts.print()

ssc.start()           // Start the computation
ssc.awaitTermination() // Wait for the computation to terminate
```

In this example, the streaming computations can be defined as operations on DStreams like 'flatMap', 'map', and 'reduceByKey' on the lines of text data. The processed data (wordCounts) is then printed out. The application is then started with 'ssc.start()', and then it waits for the streaming computation to finish with 'ssc.awaitTermination()'.

2.7 What are the various components of Spark's ecosystem?

Apache Spark's ecosystem comprises several components, each with a distinct role in data processing. Here is a list of the main components:

1. **Apache Spark Core**: This is the fundamental component and the backbone of the Spark ecosystem that gives basic functionalities like task scheduling, memory management, fault recovery, interaction with storage systems, etc.

2. **Spark SQL**: As the name suggests, Spark SQL is built to handle structured and semi-structured data and allows users to perform SQL-like queries on the data. It also supports various data sources like JSON, Hive, Parquet, and so on. Spark SQL converts these SQL queries into Spark transformations, which can be highly optimized.

3. **Spark Streaming**: This component is used for real-time data processing. You can process live data streams using Spark streaming. It provides an API for handling data streams and converts these operations into a series of batch-like operations, which are then processed by the Spark engine.

4. **Spark MLlib (Machine Learning Library)**: MLlib is Spark's built-in library used for machine learning. It is equipped with techniques for classifications, regressions, clustering, collaborative filtering, etc., and can be used on big data in a distributed processing environment.

5. **GraphX**: This is Spark's API for dealing with Graph compu-

tations. GraphX comes with several built-in graph algorithms, and users can also create their own custom graph algorithms.

6. **Cluster Manager**: Apache Spark can be run in several modes, like standalone mode, Apache Mesos, or Hadoop YARN. These managers are used for the allocation of resources to Spark applications.

Here is a diagram that depicts the Apache Spark's ecosystem:

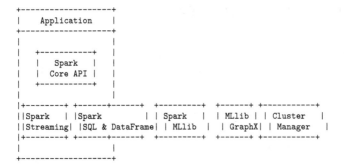

```
+--------------------+
|    Application     |
+--------------------+
|                    |
|   +-----------+    |
|   |   Spark   |    |
|   | Core API  |    |
|   +-----------+    |
|                    |
|+--------+ +------+------+  +---------+  +------+ +-----------+
||Spark   | |Spark        |  | Spark   |  | MLib | | Cluster   |
||Streaming| |SQL & DataFrame| | MLlib  |  | GraphX| | Manager   |
|+--------+ +------+------+  +---------+  +------+ +-----------+
|                    |
+--------------------+
```

This structure allows Spark to handle a wide range of workloads such as ETL jobs, batch jobs, query jobs, streaming data, machine learning, and graph processing.

2.8   How does Spark achieve fault tolerance?

Apache Spark achieves fault tolerance through a feature called Resilient Distributed Datasets (RDDs). RDDs are the fundamental data structure of Spark, distributed across the nodes in a cluster but can recover quickly if a node fails.

Fault tolerance in Spark is achieved in two ways:

1. **Lineage Information**: RDDs maintain information about their

data lineage, i.e., the series of transformations that produced the data. In the event of a data loss, Spark can recreate the RDD from its lineage information and does not need to replicate the data across multiple nodes. This is a primary way how Spark provides fault tolerance.

2. **Data Persistence**: In addition to lineage information, Spark also provides the flexibility to persist the intermediate datasets using operations like 'persist()' or 'cache()'. The RDD persistence allows the users to store frequently used RDDs or its part into memory or disk so that it can be reused across stages. This stored data is also resilient and can be recovered fast in case of any failures.

Here's a simple code example showing RDD's data lineage in Spark:

```
val data = Array(1, 2, 3, 4, 5)
val distData = sparkContext.parallelize(data)

val mappedData = distData.map(x => x * 2)
mappedData.persist()

// If any node storing `mappedData` RDD crashed,
// the RDD can be efficiently recreated using lineage information i.e.,
     distData and transformation map
mappedData.collect()
```

In the given code, 'distData' is an RDD which is created from an array data source. Another RDD 'mappedData' is then derived from 'distData' with the map transformation. If a failure occurs during the 'collect()' action on 'mappedData', Spark can easily recompute the lost data partitions of 'mappedData' because it knows the lineage of 'mappedData'.

So, if data is lost on a failed node, Spark can recreate the lost partitions of an RDD from its lineage information and that's how Spark achieves fault tolerance.

2.9   What is the role of Spark Driver?

The Spark Driver is the program that declares transformations and actions on data and submits such requests to the system. It is the central point and the entry point of the Spark Application.

Responsibilities of Spark Driver include:

1. **Creating SparkContext**: When a driver program runs, it creates a SparkContext. This SparkContext tells Spark how to access a cluster.

```
from pyspark import SparkContext
sc = SparkContext("local", "First␣App")
```

2. **Translating application code** into a directed acyclic graph (DAG) of individual tasks that get executed within an executor process.

```
data = sc.parallelize(list("Hello␣World"))
counts = data.map(lambda x: (x, 1)).reduceByKey(lambda x, y: x + y).collect()
```

3. **Scheduling tasks**: The driver schedules future tasks based on data placement. It monitors the execution of tasks and keeps track of the completed or failed tasks.

4. **Collecting Results**: It collects data back from the Spark executors to the driver program.

5. **Persisting Data**: The driver can persist RDDs to disk.

```
rdd1.persist(StorageLevel.DISK_ONLY)
```

6. **Broadcasting variables**: Spark driver sends application variables to every node in the cluster, so they can be used for performing tasks.

```
broadcastVar = sc.broadcast([1,2,3])
```

Remember, the driver program must listen and accept incoming connections from its executors throughout its lifetime. The reverse does not hold true; if the driver program exits for any reason, all executors will be terminated, and the job no longer exists in the cluster. As such, the process running the driver program needs to be machine resident with a stable and reliable network connection to the Spark executors.

2.10   What is Spark Executor?

Spark Executor is a distributed agent responsible for the execution of tasks. Each Spark Executor has its individual JVM and runs on a separate machine or container in a cluster. Every Spark application has its own executor(s). An executor stays up for the entire lifetime of a Spark application and runs tasks in multiple threads.

The tasks running on an executor share the same JVM and the same resources. They also share the same variables among them. Each executor has a dedicated heap size, which must be carefully managed. If the heap size is too small, the executor may fail due to out-of-memory errors. If it's too large, it might cause garbage collection overhead.

Below is a diagram showing the basic architecture of Spark. 'Spark-Context' is the entry point of any spark functionality. When 'Spark-Context' is created, it asks the cluster manager for resources to launch tasks. The cluster manager launches executors on the worker nodes on behalf of 'SparkContext'. 'SparkContext' sends application code (jar or Python files) to the executors. Finally, 'SparkContext' sends tasks to the executors to run.

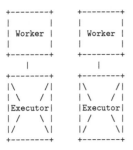

The number of executors, their cores, and the amount of memory they use are parameters that can be set when submitting a Spark application. These parameters greatly affect the performance of Spark computations.

A successful tuning of these parameters across a cluster can utilize the maximum resources which improves the overall performance of the Spark application. Mismanagement can lead to issues like out-of-memory exceptions or exceedingly long GC pauses. This is why understanding the role of Spark Executor is so crucial.

2.11   What is a Spark application?

A Spark application is an instance of SparkContext which is hosted on a Spark Cluster. This application can be used to perform computations and analysis on the data residing within the cluster. The SparkContext works as the coordinator that assigns tasks to each node in the cluster and manages all the functionalities.

The workflow of a Spark application is as follows:

1. The application is split into a series of tasks that will be distributed across the nodes in the Spark cluster.

2. Each task is executed independently by the driver program on various partitions of distributed datasets.

3. The special data structure RDD (Resilient Distributed Dataset), which is a fundamental data structure of Spark, is used to handle these distributed tasks.

4. The results are returned to the driver program upon completion of tasks.

Here is a simple Spark application in Python:

```python
from pyspark import SparkConf, SparkContext

conf = SparkConf().setAppName("My Spark App")
sc = SparkContext(conf=conf)

data = [1, 2, 3, 4, 5]
distData = sc.parallelize(data)

result = distData.reduce(lambda a, b: a + b)
print(result)
```

In this application:

1. A SparkConf object is created to hold configuration parameters for the Spark application.

2. SparkContext object 'sc' is created from SparkConf object and this represents the connection to a Spark cluster.

3. A simple Python list 'data' is parallelized into a distributed dataset 'distData'.

4. A 'reduce' operation is performed on 'distData' to add up all numbers in the list and the result is collected to the driver program.

5. The result is printed out on the driver program.

This is a simple example of a Spark application. The code is launched on a set of machines in the Spark cluster and tasks performed on the distributed dataset are carried out on these machines.

2.12   What is SparkContext?

'SparkContext' is the entry point for any Spark functionality. When we run any Spark application, a driver program starts which has a main function and Spark execution context is created – 'SparkContext'. You can think of 'SparkContext' as the connection to the Spark Cluster. Its purpose is to coordinate and to monitor the execution of tasks. All Spark applications run as independent sets of processes, coordinated by the 'SparkContext' in the driver program.

An example of initiating 'SparkContext' in Scala code:

```
import org.apache.spark.SparkContext
import org.apache.spark.SparkContext._
import org.apache.spark.SparkConf

object sparkcontext_example {
  def main(args: Array[String]) {
    val conf = new SparkConf().setAppName("SparkContext Example")
    val sc = new SparkContext(conf)
    // here you can use sc
  }
}
```

Note: You cannot have multiple 'SparkContexts' in the same JVM. You'd have to stop ('SparkContext.stop()') the current context before creating a new one.

2.13   How is Spark SQL different from traditional SQL?

Spark SQL, a component of Apache Spark, provides support for manipulation and querying of structured data, both within Spark programs and on standalone databases. It differs from traditional SQL (Structured Query Language) in several ways:

1. **Integration with Big Data Tools**: Spark SQL integrates with big data tools and supports data sources such as HBase, Cassandra, Hive, etc. Traditional SQL, on the other hand, is used on relatively

small-scale data for structured data querying mainly in relational database management systems (RDBMS).

2. **Processing Speed**: Spark SQL leverages the power of Spark to perform computations on big data, which is faster than traditional SQL running on standalone databases or RDBMS.

3. **Support for Complex Data Types**: Unlike traditional SQL, Spark SQL supports complex, nested, and schema-less data types, which are common in big data scenarios.

4. **Data Formats**: Spark SQL can process data stored in multiple formats (like Parquet, Avro, JSON, ORC, etc.) with the same performance. Traditional SQL works best with tabular, structured data in formats like CSVs, and performance may depend on the database management system.

5. **In-Memory Computing and Fault Tolerance**: Spark SQL is built upon the Spark computation engine, which supports in-memory processing and fault tolerance, providing advantages in terms of processing speed and reliability over traditional SQL.

6. **SQL and Programming Language Integration**: Spark SQL allows blending of SQL queries with Spark programs. This unification means that developers can switch seamlessly between different APIs which use either Spark data frame or Dataset APIs.

Here's an example of using Spark SQL:

```
val spark = SparkSession.builder.appName("Spark SQL basic example").config("
    spark.some.config.option", "some-value").getOrCreate()
import spark.implicits._
val df = spark.read.json("examples/src/main/resources/people.json")
df.createOrReplaceTempView("people")
val sqlDF = spark.sql("SELECT * FROM people")
sqlDF.show()
```

In this code, we first set up a SparkSession, read in a JSON file into a DataFrame, register it as a temporary table "people", and then use Spark SQL to run a SQL query on the "people" table. The result is also a DataFrame, displaying the advantages of the seamless integration between SQL and programming APIs in Spark SQL.

2.14 What are DataFrames and Datasets in Spark?

In Apache Spark, DataFrames and Datasets are distributed collection of data. They are immutable, which means once you create a DataFrame or Dataset, you cannot change it. They also ensure fault tolerance in case of any failures.

1. DataFrame:

DataFrame in Spark is a distributed collection of data organized into named columns. It is conceptually equivalent to a table in a relational database, but with richer optimizations under the hood. It provides the functionality of both RDD (Resilient Distributed Dataset) and Spark SQL with performance optimization. DataFrame API was released as an abstraction in Spark 1.3.0.

Here is a sample pseudocode to create DataFrame:

```
from pyspark.sql import SparkSession

# Create a spark session
spark = SparkSession.builder.getOrCreate()

# Define a DataFrame
df = spark.read.csv('sample.csv')

# Show the DataFrame
df.show()
```

2. Dataset:

A Dataset is a distributed collection of data with named columns and provides the same functionality as DataFrames along with the benefits of strong static types, ability to use powerful lambda functions and efficient object serialization/deserialization, which are typically helpful in JVM languages like Java and Scala. There are no Dataset APIs in Python and R, because they have dynamic typing and in these

languages, DataFrames are as efficient as Datasets. The Dataset API
was released with Spark 1.6.0.

Here is how can you create a Dataset in Scala:

```
val sparkSession = SparkSession.builder.getOrCreate()

// Define case class
case class Person(name: String, age: Int)

// Create Dataset
val dataSet = sparkSession.read.json("sample.json").as[Person]
```

DataFrame or Dataset can be inferred and specific schemas can be
defined. You can use SQL statements with them or filter data using
the languages' internal functionality. Operations with DataFrame and
DataSet are lazily evaluated, meaning the execution won't start until
an action is triggered. These features make DataFrame and DataSet
efficient and easy to use.

2.15   What is a Spark transformation?

Apache Spark transformations are functions that produce a new Resilient Distributed Dataset (RDD) from the existing one. Basically,
there are two types of transformations, Lazy transformations and Eager transformations.

Spark remains idle during the definition of transformations and only
performs actions when absolutely necessary. This property is known
as laziness of transformations. It helps optimize the overall computation process.

Let's briefly explore the two kinds of transformations.

1. Lazy Transformations: These transformations are not executed
immediately, but Spark Memorizes the transformations applied. For
example, 'map', 'flatMap', 'filter', etc.

```
data = sc.parallelize([1,2,3,4,5])
lazy_transform = data.map(lambda x: x * 2)
```

In the above example, 'map' is a lazy transformation, so no computation will happen at this step.

2. Eager Transformations: These transformations return a value to Driver program or write data to an external storage system after computation. It happens immediately after calling an action. The examples are 'count', 'collect', 'first', 'take', etc.

```
data = sc.parallelize([1,2,3,4,5])
lazy_transform = data.map(lambda x: x * 2)
eager_transform = lazy_transform.collect()
```

Here, 'collect' is an eager transformation that returns all the elements of the dataset as an array to the driver program, initiating the computation over the RDD.

With these transformations, Spark optimizes the execution using its scheduler, query optimizer, and a physical execution engine, helping to construct a Directed Acyclic Graph (DAG) for executing the transformations. So, transformations are essential building blocks, allowing data processing on Spark RDDs.

2.16   What is a Spark action?

Apache Spark operates on the principle of Lazy Evaluation, which means that computations are not executed immediately when they are defined in the program. Instead, they are recorded and executed only when an action is called. An Action in Apache Spark is a command or operation which triggers data computation and sends the result to a driver program.

Actions in Spark cause the stages (group of transformations) to be executed in the DAG Scheduler (Directed Acyclic Graph Scheduler) and return the result to the driver program or write it to an external data store.

There are various action operations available in Apache Spark. Here are few examples:

1. 'collect()': This action returns all the elements of the RDD (Resilient Distributed Datasets) as an array to the driver program. Example:

```
val rdd = sc.parallelize(Array(1,2,3,4,5))
val arrayData = rdd.collect()
```

2. 'take(n)': This action returns the first 'n' elements of the RDD. Example:

```
val rdd = sc.parallelize(Array(1,2,3,4,5))
val firstThree = rdd.take(3)
```

3. 'first()': This action returns the first element of the RDD. Example:

```
val rdd = sc.parallelize(Array(1,2,3,4,5))
val firstElement = rdd.first()
```

4. 'count()': This action returns the number of elements in the RDD. Example:

```
val rdd = sc.parallelize(Array(1,2,3,4,5))
val count = rdd.count()
```

5. 'foreach()': This action is used with function and applies the provided function to every element in the dataset. Example:

```
val rdd = sc.parallelize(Array(1,2,3,4,5))
rdd.foreach(println)
```

6. 'reduce(func)': This action aggregates the elements of the dataset using a function 'func' which takes two arguments and returns one. Example:

```
val rdd = sc.parallelize(Array(1,2,3,4,5))
val sum = rdd.reduce(_+_)
```

Please notice that actions in Apache Spark trigger the execution of transformations to compute the data. Also, they are typically expensive operations in terms of I/O and computation and should be used judiciously.

2.17   How does Spark handle memory management?

Apache Spark utilizes a layered architecture for memory management. It uses concepts of on-heap and off-heap memory storage, JVM (Java Virtual Machine) garbage collection, caching, and serialization for optimal data processing.

Below are some essential concepts related to Spark's memory management.

1.) On-Heap Memory: This is the default JVM heap memory. Each Spark executor in an application gets a certain amount of heap memory, specified by –executor-memory or spark.executor.memory. The heap memory consists of two regions: Storage Memory (for RDD caching) and Execution Memory (for computation in shuffles, joins, sorts, and aggregations).

2.) Off-Heap Memory: Spark can also use off-heap memory storage, which avoids garbage collection overhead and allows memory to be shared across different processes.

3.) Unified Memory Management: From Spark 1.6 onwards, a Unified Memory Management approach is used which combines both execution and storage into one region. The lesser-used part (either storage or execution) can borrow memory from a larger part. This is a more fluid and efficient use of available memory resources.

4.) Memory Management Tuning: To tune Spark's memory usage, you can use parameters like 'spark.memory.fraction' (to control what proportion of heap space is used for Spark memory, default is 0.6) and 'spark.memory.storageFraction' (out of the memory not reserved by 'spark.memory.fraction', how much is reserved for storage, default is 0.5).

An example of setting these parameters in a SparkConf would be:

```
val conf = new SparkConf()
  .set("spark.memory.fraction", "0.7")
  .set("spark.memory.storageFraction", "0.5")
```

5.) Garbage Collection: Spark relies on JVM garbage collection to reclaim objects stored in the heap space, which may cause pausing of processing. Garbage collection can be fine-tuned using 'spark.executor.extraJavaOptions' to reduce pauses.

6.) Serialization: To reduce memory consumption, Spark provides two serialization libraries: Java serialization and Kryo serialization. Kryo serialization is much faster and more compact than Java serialization but does not support all serializable types. You can choose your serialization library using 'spark.serializer'.

Here is an example of setting serialization method:

```
val conf = new SparkConf()
  .set("spark.serializer", "org.apache.spark.serializer.KryoSerializer")
```

In a nutshell, Spark's memory management is designed to allow high performance, with specific strategies to handle memory usage efficiently for both computation and storage. By understanding how Spark manages memory, you can effectively fine-tune the performance of your Spark applications.

2.18 What is the difference between persist() and cache() in Spark?

'persist()' and 'cache()' are methods in Apache Spark that are used to store intermediate computations. These methods can be useful in scenarios when you repeatedly need the results of a RDD (Resilient Distributed Dataset), DataFrame, or Dataset over multiple stages in a Spark job.

The main differences between 'persist()' and 'cache()' are as follows:

1. **Level of persistence**: 'persist()' method can accept a persistence level. The different persistence levels define whether the data should be stored in memory or disk or a combination of both and also whether the data should be serialized or not. This can be achieved using storage levels in Spark: 'MEMORY_ONLY', 'MEMORY_AND_DISK', 'DISK_ONLY', 'MEMORY_ONLY_SER' (Serialized), 'MEMORY_AND_DISK_SER', etc. For example:

```
import pyspark
sc = pyspark.SparkContext('local','example')
rdd = sc.parallelize(range(100))
rdd.persist(pyspark.StorageLevel.DISK_ONLY)
```

On the other hand, 'cache()' method is a shorthand for 'persist()' with default storage level 'MEMORY_AND_DISK'. In other words, 'cache()' is equivalent to 'persist(StorageLevel.MEMORY_AND_DISK)'.

```
import pyspark
sc = pyspark.SparkContext('local','example')
rdd = sc.parallelize(range(100))
rdd.cache()
```

2. **Performance**: As 'cache()' uses 'MEMORY_AND_DISK' by default, it stores the intermediate data in memory as far as it can, and spills it to disk if memory is insufficient, which can make the computation faster. But if you have a large amount of data that could not be stored in memory, 'persist()' would be a better choice as you can choose 'DISK_ONLY' or 'MEMORY_AND_DISK_SER' to avoid out-of-memory errors.

Remember both 'cache()' and 'persist()' operations are lazy in Spark, and will be executed only after an action is triggered. You should also be careful when persisting data, as it can cause the overall performance to decrease if used improperly due to the overhead of saving the data.

2.19   What is the role of a Spark Worker node?

A Spark Worker node refers to any node that can run program code within a Spark application. The main roles of a Spark Worker node are:

1. **Running Application's Tasks:** After the driver program has defined the transformations and actions on the data and divided the tasks, these tasks are sent by the Driver program to the worker nodes. The workers then run these tasks. This occurs in a distributed and parallel manner.

2. **Storing Data:** The worker nodes also store data for the Spark application. This may include the input data or the data generated by transformations. Spark can store this data in memory (for fast access) or on disk.

3. **Reporting Back to the Driver Program:** After execution of tasks, each worker node sends the results back to the driver program or stores the results to an external storage system. They also report the status of the task execution back to the Driver program.

It's important to note that Spark Worker Nodes communicate with the Spark Master node for the execution of tasks. The master node assigns tasks to the worker nodes and the worker nodes report the status of the tasks back to the master.

Here is an example in the form of a code snippet which shows a Spark application running tasks on worker nodes:

```
from pyspark import SparkConf, SparkContext

conf = SparkConf().setAppName("wordCount").setMaster("spark://master:7077") #
      setting up configuration
sc = SparkContext(conf=conf) # creating a spark context

text_file = sc.textFile("hdfs://master:9000/input/") # reading data from HDFS
counts = text_file.flatMap(lambda line: line.split("␣"))
            .map(lambda word: (word, 1))
            .reduceByKey(lambda a, b: a + b)
counts.saveAsTextFile("hdfs://master:9000/output") # saving the output to
```

HDFS

In this script, the 'flatMap', 'map' and 'reduceByKey' transformations and actions are tasks that get distributed and executed on the worker nodes. The 'textFile' and 'saveAsTextFile' commands are responsible for reading from and writing to HDFS, and this can be parallelized across worker nodes as well.

2.20 What is the difference between reduceByKey() and groupByKey() in Spark?

In Apache Spark, both 'reduceByKey()' and 'groupByKey()' are transformation operations and used to aggregate the data, but there are significant differences between them related to their performance and the manner in which they perform the tasks:

1. 'reduceByKey()': The 'reduceByKey()' function combines values with the same key using a function. The function takes two values and returns one value which can be of the same or different datatype. The transformation is executed in a way that the output preserves partitioning so that it can be used through operations like join and cogroup. Due to this, 'reduceByKey()' performs significantly better than 'groupByKey()'.

Here is a Python example:

```
rdd = sc.parallelize([('fruit', 'apple'), ('fruit', 'banana'), ('animal', '
    cat'), ('fruit', 'pear'), ('animal', 'dog')])
rdd1 = rdd.map(lambda x: (x[0], 1))
rdd2 = rdd1.reduceByKey(lambda a, b: a + b)
rdd2.collect()

# output: [('fruit', 3), ('animal', 2)]
```

'reduceByKey()' generates the pairs 'fruit' => 3 and 'animal' => 2, meaning there are 3 fruits and 2 animals.

2. 'groupByKey()': The 'groupByKey()' function groups all the values with the same key in the PairRDD. It brings all the data with the same key into the memory of a single worker machine before the processing, which may cause an out of memory issue if the dataset size is significant.

Here is a Python example:

```
rdd = sc.parallelize([('fruit', 'apple'), ('fruit', 'banana'), ('animal', '
    cat'), ('fruit', 'pear'), ('animal', 'dog')])
rdd1 = rdd.groupByKey()
rdd2 = rdd1.mapValues(list)
rdd2.collect()

# output: [('fruit', ['apple', 'banana', 'pear']), ('animal', ['cat', 'dog'])
    ]
```

After applying the 'groupByKey()' operation, we get the pairs 'fruit' => ['apple', 'banana', 'pear'] and 'animal' => ['cat', 'dog'].

In summary, while both 'reduceByKey()' and 'groupByKey()' perform similar tasks, 'reduceByKey()' is generally preferred over 'groupByKey()' due to its better performance and lesser consumption of system resources. This is because 'reduceByKey()' performs the merging operation locally on each mapper before sending results to a reducer, thereby reducing unnecessary shuffling over the network.

Chapter 3

Intermediate

3.1 How does Spark's in-memory processing enhance performance compared to Hadoop's MapReduce?

Apache Spark's in-memory processing capabilities are one of its distinct features compared to Hadoop's MapReduce. This can significantly enhance performance.

In Hadoop MapReduce, intermediate data (the output of Map jobs that is input to Reduce jobs) is stored on the disk. The Map and Reduce jobs are executed separately – Map jobs are scheduled, executed, and their output stored to disk. Then Reduce jobs are scheduled and executed. This means that data is written to and read from disk between the execution of the Map and Reduce tasks, which can lead to substantial lag, described as "disk I/O," considering disk speeds are significantly slower than memory speeds.

On the contrary, Apache Spark's design principle is based on 'Resilient Distributed Datasets' (RDDs) which can be cached across com-

41

puting nodes in a cluster. Intermediate data generated in Spark can be stored in memory as RDDs, and can be reused across multiple stages in computations. For example:

```
data = sc.parallelize([1, 2, 3, 4, 5])
cached_data = data.map(t => (t, 1)).cache()
```

In these lines of code, an RDD is created from a basic set, then mapped into a tuple and cached in memory for further operations.

Spark's in-memory capability is particularly useful when handling iterative algorithms and caching intermediate data, which is common in machine learning algorithms, graph processing, etc.

However, it's also important to note that storing too much data in-memory can lead to issues. To prevent this, Spark provides a storage level API that allows users to control its persist method (e.g., persisting data to the disk, persisting data to off-heap memory, etc.).

Overall, by keeping data in memory, Spark reduces the need for time-consuming I/O operations and speeds up processing times, which are crucial for carrying out big data analytics, machine learning tasks, and other such tasks where data needs to be frequently retrieved.

3.2   Explain the differences between narrow and wide transformations in Spark.

In the context of Apache Spark, transformations are operations on RDDs, DataFrames, and DataSets that create a new data set from an existing one. Transformations, in Spark, are categorized as Narrow transformation and Wide transformation.

1. Narrow Transformations: In Narrow transformation, all elements that are required to compute the records in single partition live in the single partition of parent RDD. A narrow transformation does not require the data to be shuffled across the partitions. Example of

narrow transformations include 'map()', 'filter()', and 'union()'.

Example:

```
val lines = sparkContext.textFile("path_to_file")
val words = lines.flatMap(line => line.split(" "))
```

In this example 'textFile()' method will create an RDD, and the 'flatMap()' is a narrow transformation on this RDD, which does not require shuffling.

2. Wide Transformations: In Wide transformation, all elements that are required to compute the records in the single partition may live in many partitions of parent RDD. A wide transformation requires the data to be shuffled across multiple partitions. Examples of wide transformations include 'groupByKey()', 'reduceByKey()', 'join()', 'cogroup()', and 'distinct()'.

Example:

```
val countWords = words.map(word => (word, 1)).reduceByKey(_ + _)
```

In this example, 'map()' is a narrow transformation whereas 'reduce-ByKey()' is a wide transformation. 'reduceByKey()' will cause a shuffle of data to bring the same keys onto the same partition for the reduction operation.

The key difference between narrow and wide transformations lies in whether a shuffle operation is caused. Narrow transformations have the benefit of running more quickly because they don't require a costly shuffle, however, they may not be practical if data needs to be organized across partitions. Wide transformations, on the other hand, do require a shuffle, which can be more time-consuming, but allows for broader data organization and grouping.

3.3   What are the different storage levels in Spark?

In Apache Spark, the computation is done in memory and over the network. RDDs are fundamental data structures of Spark which are an immutable collection of objects that compute on the different node of the cluster. Spark uses Caching and Persistence for storing the interim data that can be reused.

In Spark transformations are categorized into two- transformations resulting in narrow dependency (we call it Narrow transformation) and wide dependency (we call it wide transformation). With narrow transformation, all elements that are required to compute the records in a single partition live in the same partition of parent RDD. A single stage can consist of multiple narrow transformations. With wide transformations, all elements that are required to compute the records in a single partition may live in many partitions of parent RDD. Several stages in a job are as a result of wide transformations.

There are five different storage levels in Apache Spark:

1. **MEMORY_ONLY**: In this level, RDDs are stored only in memory. This is the most CPU-efficient option, allowing operations on the RDDs to run as fast as possible. If the RDD does not fit into memory, some partitions will not be cached and will have to be re-computed on the fly each time they're needed.

2. **MEMORY_AND_DISK**: In this level, RDDs are stored in memory first, if the RDD doesn't fit into memory then it stores the RDD into disk.

3. **MEMORY_ONLY_SER (Java & Scala)**: In this level, RDDs are stored in memory by serializing the objects into a binary format, and then storing them. This can be more space-efficient than deserialized Java objects, especially when fast serialization library is used.

4. **MEMORY_AND_DISK_SER (Java & Scala)**: Similar to

MEMORY_ONLY_SER but spill partitions that don't fit into memory to disk instead of recomputing them on the fly each time they're needed.

5. **DISK_ONLY**: In this level, Store the RDD partitions only on disk.

6. There are also off-heap options (OFF_HEAP) options available from spark 2.3 onwards, which allows RDDs to be cached in serialized format in Tachyon's memory space, allowing spark to manage its own memory more efficiently, freeing up more resources for other operations.

You can see a summary in the table below:

Storage Level	Space Used	CPU Used	In-Memory	On Disk	Serialized
MEMORY_ONLY	High	Low	Yes	No	No
MEMORY_AND_DISK	High	Medium	Some	Some	No
MEMORY_ONLY_SER	Low	High	Yes	No	Yes
MEMORY_AND_DISK_SER	Low	High	Some	Some	Yes
DISK_ONLY	Low	High	No	Yes	Yes

- *Space Used*: how much space the stored data will occupy.

- *CPU Used*: impact of storing data on the Computational cost.

- *In-Memory*: partitions are stored in memory.

- *On-Disk*: partitions are stored on disk.

- *Serialized*: whether the data is stored in serialized format.

Finally, the storage level can be set using the persist or cache methods. For example, you can set the storage level on an RDD using rdd.persist(StorageLevel.MEMORY_AND_DISK_SER), which will store the RDD in memory and disk in serialized format. If no specific storage level is specified, then persist() method will use MEMORY_ONLY level by default.

3.4 How can you minimize data shuffling in Spark?

Data shuffling is the process of redistributing data so that it is grouped differently across partitions. This operation is often necessary for certain operations but can be quite expensive in terms of computation and network communication.

There are two types of transformations in Spark: transformations that induce shuffling and those that don't. The latter are known as Narrow transformations (e.g., map(), filter(), and union()) and the former are known as Wide transformations (e.g., groupByKey(), reduceByKey(), join(), cogroup(), and repartition()).

Shuffling of data in wide transformation is expensive because it involves disk I/O, serialization, and network I/O. However, in certain scenarios, shuffling is inevitable.

To minimize shuffling, we can perform certain optimizations:

1. **Avoid operations that cause data shuffling.** Avoiding operations such as groupByKey() when there is a need to group data in an RDD, instead, consider using reduceByKey() or foldByKey(), which perform a map-side combine before the shuffle, and substantially decrease the amount of data shuffled.

2. **Use transformations that exploit the fact that data is already partitioned.** Spark provides transformations such as mapPartitions(), which can be more efficient because they provide an iterator to the data, hence you don't need to create an object for each element in your data.

3. **Choose the right operations:**

- Always use 'reduceByKey()' over 'groupByKey()', as 'reduceByKey()' performs local aggregation first before the shuffling which helps in reducing lot of network I/O.

- Use 'join()' operation intelligently. If one of the RDDs is considerably smaller, then use 'broadcast()' variable to send smaller RDD to all the nodes with bigger RDD.

4. **Manually partition the data:** You can use transformations such as 'repartition()' and 'partitionBy()' to manually control data partitioning based on your use case.

In essence, it's about understanding your data and being smart with your transformations. Know your data, know your operations, and optimize accordingly.

3.5 Describe the life cycle of a Spark job from its beginning to its end.

The life cycle of a Spark job involves several stages from its start till completion.

1. **Creation of RDD (Resilient Distributed Dataset):** The first step in the life cycle of a Spark job is the creation of RDDs. An RDD, which stands for 'Resilient Distributed Dataset', is an immutable distributed collection of data. These are the fundamental data structures of Spark. RDDs can be created from data stored in storage systems like Hadoop Distributed File System (HDFS), local file systems, etc.

```
rdd = spark.textFile("/path/to/textfile")
```

2. **Transformation of RDD:** The next stage in the life cycle of a Spark job are transformations. Transformations are operations on RDDs that create a new RDD. They are lazily evaluated which means that they are not immediately executed when invoked, instead Spark records the transformations applied to some base dataset (e.g. a file). Some examples of transformation commands are 'map()', 'filter()', 'union()', etc.

```
filtered_rdd = rdd.filter(lambda x: "error" in x)
```

3. **Performed Action:** After the transformations, the next stage
is to perform an action. Actions are RDD operations that produce
non-RDD values. They materialize a value in a Spark program which
triggers the execution using lineage graph to load the data into original RDD, carry out all intermediate transformations and return the
final results to Driver program or write it out to file system. Some
examples of actions are 'count()', 'first()', 'collect()', etc.

```
errors_count = filtered_rdd.count()
```

After an action is called, Spark submits the job to the Spark scheduler.
The scheduler divides the job into stages. A stage consists of tasks
based on the transformations that can be carried out together. Then,
it executes the tasks on Spark executors.

4. **Scheduler:** When the driver runs, it converts a logical execution plan to physical execution plan and submits jobs to an underlying
cluster manager. The job is divided into stages of tasks. A new stage
is created for every shuffle operation. The Directed Acyclic Graph
(DAG) scheduler pipelines operators together.

5. **Task execution:** In each stage, tasks are spawned. Each task
represents a unit of work that will be sent to one executor. Spark tries
to stick tasks that operate on the same partition (i.e., the same chunk
of data) together in the same stage. The tasks are then executed on
the executors.

6. **Results:** The results of the tasks are sent back to the driver.
If an action was called to return results to the driver, the results of
the action are collected and returned.

```
print('Number of lines with "error": %s' % errors_count)
```

In summary, the life cycle of a Spark job is a series of transformations followed by an action. It starts with creating RDDs, applying
transformations, performing an action, scheduling of tasks, execution
of tasks and then returning the results. Throughout these stages, the
Spark scheduler and executor play a vital role.

3.6 What is the significance of partitions in Spark?

Partitions in Apache Spark play a pivotal role in distributed computing. They are integral chunks of a dataset that is stored in a distributed system or in simple terms, smaller logical divisions of data. This data can be a distributed collection of objects (like an RDD), a DataFrame, Dataset or a file in HDFS, a local file, or any data source that can be viewed as a distributed collection.

In Apache Spark, data is actually processed in partitions. Any operation on a RDD or DataFrame, are actually operations on its partitions.

Here's why partitions are significant:

1. Parallelism: Data is split across the nodes in partitions, and operations are performed on each partition independently and in parallel. The Spark or MapReduce job's speed then depends on the number of partitions. More the partitions, better the performance.

2. Resource Utilization: Proper partitioning of data ensures effective utilization of available resources. This could also improve the processing speed.

3. Minimizing data shuffling: Effective partitioning ensures that data required for processing is close to the executor. This provides a boost in processing and minimizes network IO.

4. Fail recovery: As each partitioned data is stored in node, failure of a node need not cause the entire system to collapse. The loss would only be a component of data which could be recovered because of RDD's resilient nature.

By default, Spark tries to read data into an RDD from the nodes that are close to it. Because of data locality in Spark, it is often very fast and works well without any specific settings.

One key aspect when working with partitions: an operation known as transformations in Apache Spark is lazily evaluated, meaning the execution doesn't start right away. They are computed on demand and returned as a new RDD. Transformations are further classified to narrow and wide transformations. Narrow transformation means data required to compute the records in a single partition live in the same partition of the parent RDD. Examples of such transformations are map(), filter(). Wide transformations require the data from all partitions. Examples are groupByKey(), reduceByKey() etc.

Here's a code snippet to show how you can check and manipulate the number of partitions:

```
# Create a new RDD
rdd = sc.parallelize(range(10))
# Check the number of partitions
print(rdd.getNumPartitions())
# Increase the number of partitions
rdd_modified = rdd.repartition(10)
print(rdd_modified.getNumPartitions())
```

In the above code, 'sc.parallelize(range(10))' creates a new RDD, 'rdd.getNumPartitions()' fetches the current number of partitions, and 'rdd.repartition(10)' increases the number of partitions.

3.7   How do you handle node failures in Spark during data processing?

Apache Spark provides a fault tolerance feature using the Resilient Distributed Datasets (RDD) abstraction. An RDD in Spark is an immutable distributed collection of objects. Each dataset in RDD is divided into logical partitions, which may be computed on different nodes of the cluster.

If a node running Spark fails during a computation, Spark can recover the lost computation on that node by recalculating the lost partitions of the RDD. This is because the metadata of RDD, including the lineage information (i.e., the sequence of transformations used to build the dataset), is maintained in the driver program.

Let's take an example where we have an RDD 'rdd1' and we apply a map function on it to create 'rdd2' and then a filter function is applied to 'rdd2' to create 'rdd3'.

```
rdd1 = sc.parallelize(data)
rdd2 = rdd1.map(function1)
rdd3 = rdd2.filter(function2)
```

If a node fails after the filter function is applied, Spark can recover 'rdd3' by re-computing 'rdd2' for the lost partitions and then applying the filter function. This doesn't require recomputation of unaffected partitions.

However, the recovery method depends on the type of operators used in the RDD lineage:

- Transformations in Spark are categorized into narrow and wide dependencies (referring to transformations that do not require data to be shuffled across partitions, and those that do, respectively).

- For narrow transformations, like 'map' and 'filter' (which work on single partition), recovery of any lost partition can be achieved by re-computing that specific partition on the parent RDD. This provides a faster recovery mechanism as only the lost partition needs to be computed.

- For wide dependencies, like 'groupByKey' and 'reduceByKey' (operations where data is shuffled across multiple partitions), Spark provides checkpointing facility where intermediate data can be stored in reliable storage (like HDFS). This is useful when the lineage chain is too long and hence recovery time is high.

```
rdd1.checkpoint()
```

This checkpointing process is lazy, meaning the actual checkpointing does not happen until an action is called.

In a nutshell, Spark provides robust fault tolerance mechanism which can handle node failures during data processing by using the combination of RDD's lineage information and checkpointing facility.

3.8   What is Spark's Catalyst optimizer?

Apache Spark's Catalyst Optimizer is a powerful, integrated query optimizer in Spark SQL that encompasses a broad set of transformation rules aimed at both logical and physical plan optimization. This optimizer was introduced to enhance the Spark's SQL functionalities in an highly efficient and adaptable way.

The Catalyst optimizer was designed with two key purposes:

1. Enhance the extensibility of Apache Spark: It allows external developers to add new optimization techniques and enables other features like advanced statistics supported in the future.

2. Improve the query execution speed: It uses advanced programming language features (in Scala) to build an extensible query optimizer.

The Catalyst Optimizer goes through following stages to optimize an execution plan:

1. Analyzing a logical plan to resolve references: It starts with a SQL or DataFrame/Dataset and then converts that into an unresolved logical plan where it tries to resolve the attributes of the relation used in the SQL based on the schema.

2. Logical plan optimization: It applies standard optimization rules like predicate pushdown, projection pruning etc., on the logical plan.

3. Physical planning: The logical plan with optimization rules applied is further converted into one or more Physical plans.

4. Code generation to compile part of the query to Java bytecode. It generates compact bytecode for expressions and then uses 'WholeStageCodegenExec' operator to collapse the entire query to a single function thereby, improving CPU cache hit rate.

Here is an example of predicate pushdown, one of the commonly applied optimization techniques:

Suppose you have a DataFrame 'df' with columns 'id' and 'desc' and you execute the following command:

```
df.filter("id =_10").select("desc")
```

Without any optimization, Spark would first load all the data in 'df', filter out rows where 'id' is not 10, then drop the 'id' column from these entries. But Catalyst sees it can reorder the operations more efficiently: it first narrows down rows where 'id' is 10, then loads only 'desc' for these entries.

Overall, the Catalyst Optimizer significantly optimizes compute resources and boosts the execution speed, making Spark more efficient.

3.9   How does Spark integrate with Hadoop?

Apache Spark can run on top of a Hadoop Cluster utilizing YARN (Yet Another Resource Negotiator) for resource management and HDFS (Hadoop Distributed File System) for storage. It can also process data stored in other supported storage systems, like HBase, Cassandra, etc.

1. **Hadoop Cluster Mode with YARN:**

Spark can be configured to run on a Hadoop Cluster that uses YARN as the resource manager. In this setup, Spark applications run as YARN applications. Resource allocation, scheduling, and execution of Spark tasks are handled by YARN.

Here is an example of how to submit a Spark job using the Spark submit utility in YARN client mode:

```
./bin/spark-submit --class org.apache.spark.examples.SparkPi
  --master yarn
  --deploy-mode client
  --executor-memory 1g
  --num-executors 3
  /path/to/examples.jar
  10
```

In this example, 'spark-submit' is the utility to submit Spark jobs, '–master yarn' instructs Spark to use YARN as the cluster manager, '–deploy-mode client' informs Spark to run the driver program locally as a client to the cluster.

2. **HDFS - Hadoop Distributed File System:**

Spark can also integrate with HDFS, which is a distributed file system designed to hold very large amounts of data (terabytes or even petabytes), and provide high-throughput access to this information. It's part of the Hadoop project.

Spark can use HDFS as a distributed storage system to maintain its data. It can read/write data from/to HDFS, which enables it to work efficiently on a large dataset distributed across multiple nodes.

Here is an example of how to read data from HDFS in Spark:

```
val sc = new SparkContext("local", "app")
val fileRDD = sc.textFile("hdfs://namenode:port/path/to/file")
```

In this example, 'sc.textFile' is pointing to a file (or files in a directory) in HDFS. Spark would then load this data distributed across the nodes.

So, the integration of Spark with Hadoop allows Spark to utilize the resource management capabilities of YARN and distributed storage capabilities of HDFS, which is particularly important when you need to process large datasets in a distributed manner. As Hadoop is often used in big data environments, this integration extends the usability of Spark in these contexts.

3.10   Explain the concept of lineage in Spark.

Lineage in Apache Spark is a concept related to the way Spark handles data loss and recovery. It is actually a form of RDD's (Resilient Distributed Datasets) fault tolerance. Essentially, lineage information is metadata about how an RDD is derived from other datasets.

In case of any data loss or damage, Spark reconstructs the lost partitions of the RDDs from this lineage information. The lineage graph
consists of a series of transformations (transformations are operations
in Spark that produce an RDD, like map(), filter(), reduce()) that can
be re-computed or replayed on the base data. The RDD transformations are essentially a series of steps, or computational instructions,
to go from the raw data to the processed data.

Here is an example of a sequence of transformations:

```
val textFile = spark.textFile("hdfs://...")
val counts = textFile.flatMap(line => line.split("␣"))
             .map(word => (word, 1))
             .reduceByKey(_ + _)
counts.saveAsTextFile("hdfs://...")
```

In this example, 'textFile', 'counts' are all RDDs and they contain
information about their lineage. For instance, 'counts' know that it
came from a 'flatMap', 'map', and 'reduceByKey' transformation on
'textFile'.

The benefit of this is two-fold:

1. Efficiency: By using lineage, Spark reduces the amount of data
that needs to be stored, and instead focuses on the process to recreate
the data. This is much more efficient especially in big data scenarios
where data itself could be huge.

2. Fault Tolerance: When data is lost in Spark, thanks to the knowledge of the lineage of the RDD, it doesn't have to start from scratch.
Instead, it re-computes or replays only those steps that are necessary
to rebuild the lost data.

Intermediate data is the data generated by transformations made on
RDDs. The computations of Spark transformations contribute to
the creation of intermediate data. In transformations, a new RDD
is created from an existing one. The intermediate data helps Spark
to optimize its operations through a process known as pipelining.

This can save substantial time and computation resources, improving Spark's overall performance.

3.11   How can you achieve data locality in Spark?

Data locality is the process of moving the computation close to where the actual data resides on the node, instead of moving large amounts of data over to computation. This can significantly improve the overall processing time.

In Spark, different levels of data locality can be defined based on the data location. Spark has 5 levels for data locality, which are -

1. PROCESS_LOCAL: Data resides in the same JVM as the running computation. This is the best scenario for data locality.

2. NODE_LOCAL: Data resides on the same node but in a different JVM. It's a little more expensive than PROCESS_LOCAL but still a good scenario.

3. NO_PREF: Location doesn't matter.

4. RACK_LOCAL: Data is on the same rack of servers. This scenario is costly because we would need to move the data between the servers on the same rack

5. ANY: Data is elsewhere on the network. This is the worst case and it leads to higher data processing times due to network latency.

Apache Spark schedules the tasks based on data locality. Ideally, it attempts to schedule the task on a node containing the block of data the task needs to compute on. If it's unable to schedule it in a node, it goes to the next level of hierarchy i.e., NODE_LOCAL and so on.

In order to increase data locality in Spark, one must take care of the following aspects:

- Try to use transformation operations (like map, filter, etc.), not action operations as much as possible, because action operations cause shuffling of data which impacts data locality.

- Minimize the amount of data shuffling as it creates a lot of network overhead, leading to poor data locality.

- Tune the parameter 'spark.locality.wait' in Spark configuration. This property defines how long Spark waits to launch a data-localized task. By default, it's set to 3s. If you're seeing poor locality, you may want to increase this value.

For example, increasing it to a higher value like below would allow Spark to wait longer for data locality:

```
sparkConf.set("spark.locality.wait", "10s")
```

Also, the data storage format and organization play key roles in achieving good data locality, so efficient partitioning of data and its organization must be a priority.

3.12 What are accumulators in Spark? Provide a use case.

Accumulators in Apache Spark are a type of shared variable that can be used to update the values of variables in parallel while executing. The updates to these variables are only added through an associative and commutative operation. Spark natively supports accumulators of numeric types, and programmers can add support for new types.

Accumulators are helpful when we need to perform operations like sum or maximum on RDDs. They are written-only variables which are initialized once and can be updated through an associative operation.

Let's take a Python code example to demonstrate how we can use accumulators:

```
from pyspark import SparkContext

sc = SparkContext("local", "accumulator app")
num = sc.accumulator(10) # creating accumulator variable and initializing
    with 10

def f(x):
    global num
    num+=x # incrementing accumulator variable

rdd = sc.parallelize([20, 30, 40, 50]) # creating an RDD
rdd.foreach(f) # applying foreach operation on rdd

final = num.value # getting accumulator value
print("Accumulated value is -> %i" % (final))
```

In this code example, an accumulator variable 'num' is initialized with value 10, and for each element in RDD, that element is added to the 'num' using 'foreach' operation of RDD.

Before the 'foreach' operation, 'num' was 10, after the operation, it becomes 150 because 20, 30, 40 and 50 are added to it.

Accumulators can have several use-cases:

1. **Global counters**: Just like Hadoop, we can use Spark accumulators for making global counters.

2. **Computing sum or total**: In the above example, we have used Spark accumulator to compute total.

3. **Data quality checks**: Accumulators can also be used for data quality checks. For example, we can create an accumulator for malformed records and increment it whenever we come across any malformed record. This will give us the number of bad records in our data.

3.13 What are broadcast variables? Why are they used?

Broadcast variables in Apache Spark are read-only shared variables that are cached and distributed on each machine rather than sending a copy of it along with the tasks. They are used to increase the efficiency of joins between small and large RDDs, lookup tables, and other similar operations.

Broadcast variables help in storing a lookup table inside the memory which enhances the retrieval efficiency when compared to an RDD lookup(). In Spark, creating a broadcast variable is achieved using the broadcast function from a Spark Context sc.broadcast().

Here's a simple example:

```
# Create a broadcast variable.
broadcastVar = sc.broadcast([1, 2, 3])

# Access the value.
broadcastVar.value
```

In the code snippet above,

- We start by creating a broadcast variable using 'sc.broadcast()'. This distributes the variable's value to all the nodes, where it's stored in the cache.

- Accessing the value of the broadcasted variable is done through 'broadcastVar.value'.

The reason for using broadcast variables is to save the cost of transmitting the data over the network again and again. They are particularly useful when data is used across multiple stages in your Spark jobs, especially when the data is large.

Consider a situation where you're performing a join operation between a small DataFrame and a large DataFrame: the smaller DataFrame would be copied for each partition of the larger DataFrame if it's not broadcasted. Broadcasting the smaller DataFrame would mean it only needs to be sent over the network once and can be reused across multiple stages and tasks throughout your job, making the whole operation much more efficient.

3.14 How is lazy evaluation beneficial in Spark?

Lazy evaluation in Spark means that the execution won't start until an action is triggered. In Spark, the transformations are lazy, meaning that they don't compute their results right away. Instead, they just remember the transformations applied to some base data set (e.g., a file). When an action requires some dataset to be produced, Spark computes the dataset. This approach might seem unusual at first, but it brings significant advantages, mainly:

1. Efficiency Enhancement: The system automatically determines the order of computation that minimizes the total cost. For example, consider a task that involves reading some data from the disk, filtering out most of it based on a predicate, and then aggregating the results. If Spark evaluated these tasks eagerly in the order they are written, it would read all data from the disk first, wasting lots of time and bandwidth, even though most of it is discarded by filtering. With lazy evaluation, Spark waits until the final result is requested before executing any computation, making the whole process more efficient.

2. Reduced Computation: The lazy evaluation strategy contributes to reducing the total computation done on the data. If, for example, you run a Spark transformation to fetch some data and then another operation to select only specific items from the fetched data, Spark will combine these operations and perform them all at once when the actual action is triggered. This can save a lot of computational effort and time.

3. Pipelining: With lazy evaluation, many transformations are grouped together and computed in a single pass over the data, which can significantly improve performance. This is also known as pipelining.

A simple example in PySpark may look like this:

```
data = spark.textFile("file.txt") # Spark only records how to load file
lines = data.filter(lambda line: "spark" in line) # Spark only records the
    use of filter
spark_lines = lines.count() # Now Spark loads the data, computes the filter,
    and counts the lines
```

In the above code, 'textFile' and 'filter' are transformations, they only record how to compute the data, but the actual computation doesn't start until 'count' (an action) is called. This lazy evaluation strategy enables Spark to optimize the overall data processing workflow, which results in improved performance.

3.15 What are the different cluster managers supported by Spark?

Apache Spark supports three types of cluster managers:

1. **Standalone Deploy Mode**: This is the simplest among all. Here Spark comes with its own built-in cluster manager where you can manage and distribute your resources. You do not need to install any separate cluster manager for it. For example, you can deploy a Spark application in standalone mode by just using a script provided by Spark, './sbin/start-master.sh'.

2. **Apache Mesos**: Apache Mesos is a cluster manager that provides efficient resource isolation and sharing across distributed applications. Spark can be configured to run on Mesos and because of Mesos architecture, it can also run other applications alongside Spark. For Mesos, you need to configure the Spark properties to point to the Mesos master by using

```
spark.master=mesos://HOST:5050
```

3. **Hadoop YARN** (Yet Another Resource Negotiator): This is
the cluster manager for Hadoop 2 and is a standard for distributed
data processing. Spark can run on YARN, allowing you to easily use
it alongside existing Hadoop deployments. For YARN, you need to
configure the Spark properties to point to Yarn by using

```
spark.master=yarn
```

The main advantage of running Spark on YARN is the ability to
dynamically share and centrally configure the same pool of cluster
resources between all frameworks that run on YARN.

4. **Kubernetes**: Apache Spark also has native Kubernetes support since Spark 2.3 version. Kubernetes is an open-source system
for automating the deployment, scaling, and managing of application
containers. It provides excellent features like scaling the number of
worker nodes through Kubectl.

To run Spark with Kubernetes, you need to configure the Spark properties to point to the Kubernetes master using

```
spark.master=k8s://https://<k8s-apiserver-host>:<k8s-apiserver-port>
```

Each of these has its own advantages, and the choice between these
should be based on the project requirements.

3.16   Explain the differences between saveAs-TextFile() and saveAsSequenceFile().

The 'saveAsTextFile()' and 'saveAsSequenceFile()' are actions in Apache
Spark that are used to save the RDD data into a file. RDD (Resilient
Distributed Datasets) is the fundamental data structure of Apache
Spark which is an immutable distributed collection of objects.

saveAsTextFile()

The 'saveAsTextFile()' method is used to save RDD data into text files inside a directory with each partition as a separate file.

For example, if we have the following RDD:

```
val rdd = sc.parallelize(Array("apple", "banana", "cherry"))
```

We can save this RDD to text file as follows:

```
rdd.saveAsTextFile("path/to/directory")
```

Each element in the RDD will be converted to its string representation and stored as a line of text. It is often used when the RDD is small enough to fit on a single machine, and you want to read it as a text file.

saveAsSequenceFile()

On the other hand, 'saveAsSequenceFile()' is used to save RDDs as SequenceFiles. SequenceFile is a popular Hadoop file format that stores key-value pairs. It is often used for intermediate data storage in MapReduce jobs.

For 'saveAsSequenceFile', your RDD should be in the form of key-value pairs, because SequenceFiles are structured as key-value pairs, both of which are Writable. In case the RDD is not in key-value pair form, you need to convert it.

Here is an example:

```
val rdd = sc.parallelize(Array(("apple", 1), ("banana", 2), ("cherry", 3)))
```

And here's how we save it as a SequenceFile:

```
rdd.saveAsSequenceFile("path/to/directory")
```

In summary, the primary differences between 'saveAsTextFile()' and 'saveAsSequenceFile()' are:

1. 'saveAsTextFile()' saves the data of RDD in text format, whereas

'saveAsSequenceFile()' uses the SequenceFile format from Hadoop which is a binary key-value pair.

2. While using 'saveAsSequenceFile()', RDD should be in key-value pair format.

3. 'saveAsTextFile()' results in a human-readable file while 'save-AsSequenceFile()' results in a binary file that's not easily readable by humans but can have performance benefits in terms of size and speed.

Please note that SequenceFile format is only available in Spark running on Hadoop clusters and not for other cluster management systems.

3.17 How do you handle large broadcast variables in Spark?

Broadcast variables allow Spark to keep a read-only variable cached on each machine, rather than shipping a copy of it with tasks. They can be used to give every node a copy of a large input dataset. This can be very useful when tasks performed by Spark require a large common dataset to be available on all the nodes.

However, if the dataset is very large, storing it as a broadcast variable might consume too much memory, which may lead to an OutOfMemoryError. To handle large broadcast variables, you can use the following strategies:

1. **Avoid broadcasting large variables**: Instead of broadcasting large datasets which can consume a lot of memory, consider computing them in a distributed manner. For example, if you need to broadcast a large dataset for a join operation, consider using a distributed version of the join, such as a skewed join or a sort-merge join.

2. **Tune spark.broadcast.blockSize**: The blockSize controls the size of each piece of the broadcast variable. Increasing blockSize might help in reducing memory consumption. However, take caution as increasing blockSize too much might lead to large network transfers.

3. **Use more efficient data structures**: Use optimized data structures for storage of the broadcast variables. For instance, you can keep your data in an array instead of a list or a linked list. This can better utilize the memory and reduce memory consumption.

4. **Use Tachyon**: Tachyon is a memory-centric distributed storage system enabling reliable data sharing at memory-speed across cluster frameworks, such as Spark and Hadoop. Tachyon can be used to store broadcast variables, thereby alleviating memory pressure on Spark.

Here's an example showing how to create a broadcast variable.

```
# Create an RDD from a list of integers
data = sc.parallelize(list(range(1, 10001)))

# Create a broadcast variable
broadcastVar = sc.broadcast(data.collect())
```

In this example, an RDD is created from a list of integers and the RDD is then collected to the driver and broadcasted. Note that calling '.collect()' on an RDD can be resource-consuming, especially if the RDD is large. The above example works for small RDDs, but for large RDDs, consider using other techniques as discussed above.

3.18   What is speculative execution in Spark?

Speculative execution in Apache Spark is a significant feature related to job execution. In distributed computing tasks, sometimes due to network issues, hardware problems, or due to straggler tasks (tasks that run slower than others), job execution can get significantly delayed. These situations could dramatically impact the overall performance of Spark jobs.

That's where speculative execution steps in. It's a fault-tolerant feature that takes care of slow machine issues (not system failures). When speculative execution is enabled (by setting "spark.speculation" to true), Spark identifies the tasks that are running slower than expected (stragglers) and starts a duplicate copy of them on other nodes.

So now, both the original and the speculative tasks are running in parallel. Whichever task finishes first, its results are accepted, and the other one gets killed. This strategy helps in minimizing the impact of slow nodes on the overall duration of the job execution in Spark.

```
sparkConf.set("spark.speculation", True)
```

However, turning on speculative execution does come with some overhead. Identifying slow tasks, launching extra tasks, and keeping track of task execution on multiple nodes all take up resources. Therefore, it's advisable to enable speculative execution only when necessary.

3.19   Describe the difference between coalesce() and repartition() in Spark.

In Apache Spark, 'coalesce()' and 'repartition()' methods are used to modify the partitioning of the Resilient Distributed Dataset (RDD)/ DataFrame/Dataset.

The 'coalesce()' function reduces the number of partitions in an RDD, DataFrame, or Dataset by combining data on the few original partitions with new fewer partitions. 'coalesce()' helps avoid performing a full reshuffle of all the data and can save resources when reducing the number of partitions. However, keep in mind that 'coalesce()' only allows shuffling downward. This means it can reduce the number of partitions but can't increase them.

An example of 'coalesce()' usage can be as follows:

```
val df = spark.range(0, 20)
val dfCoalesce = df.coalesce(2)
```

Here, 'df.coalesce(2)' reduces the number of partitions in the DataFrame 'df' to 2.

The 'repartition()' function can increase or decrease the number of partitions in an RDD, DataFrame, or Dataset. 'repartition()' does a full shuffle of the data and creates new partitions with data that's distributed evenly. Unlike 'coalesce()', 'repartition()' can increase the number of partitions.

An example of 'repartition()' usage is as follows:

```
val df = spark.range(0, 20)
val dfRepartitioned = df.repartition(5)
```

Here, 'df.repartition(5)' changes the number of partitions in the DataFrame 'df' to 5.

In summary, the primary difference between the two is that 'coalesce()' provides a simpler way to decrease the number of partitions while preserving the existing data partitioning and avoiding a full data shuffle, whereas 'repartition()' performs a full data shuffle and evenly distributes data across the network, and it can be used to increase or decrease the number of partitions. You would choose to use 'repartition()' if you want to increase the number of partitions or if you require a distributed, evenly balanced dataset.

3.20 How do you handle skewed data in Spark?

Skewed data in Spark refers to a scenario where one or few partitions have more data compared to others. This results in some tasks taking longer time than others which eventually leads to overall slow job execution time. This can happen during stages of transformations like groupByKey, reduceByKey, join, cogroup etc.

There are several ways to handle skewed data in Spark:

1. **Salting**: Salting is a technique where we add a random prefix to the key so that the output will be evenly distributed across all the reducers. This way the skewed key will also get evenly distributed and no reducer will be overloaded.

Example:

```
# Adding suffix to keys
rdd1 = rdd1.map(lambda (x, y): (str(x)+"_"+str(random.randint(0, 9)), y))

# Running reduceByKey operation
rdd1.reduceByKey(func)
```

2. **Splitting skewed keys**: Another approach is to identify the skewed keys and then split them into multiple keys. This would ensure that the load can be evenly distributed across multiple tasks.

Example:

```
# Splitting skewed keys
rdd1 = rdd1.flatMap(lambda (x, y): [(str(x)+'_'+str(i), y) for i in range(10)]
    if x in skewed_keys else [(x, y)])

# Running reduceByKey operation
rdd1.reduceByKey(func)
```

3. **Using reduceByKey instead of groupByKey**: When transforming pair RDDs where each key has many values, 'reduceByKey' works much better than 'groupByKey' as it combines output with a common key on each partition before shuffling the data.

4. **Increasing the number of partitions**: By default, Spark sets the number of partitions based on our cluster. However, if we have skewed data, we may need to increase the number to reduce the computation that each task needs to perform. We can do this by using 'repartition' or 'coalesce'.

Example:

```
# Increasing number of partitions
rdd1 = rdd1.repartition(100)
```

5. **Using Spark's skew join optimization (available in Spark 3.0 and

later)**: Spark has built-in optimization for skewed joins. Skew join
optimization handles the skew in the data by splitting the skewed
partition into smaller parts and merging the non-skewed data into
fewer partitions.

```
spark.conf.set("spark.sql.adaptive.enabled", "true")
spark.conf.set("spark.sql.adaptive.skewJoin.enabled", ""true
```

It's important to note that handling skewed data involves careful
analysis of your data and the transformations used.

Chapter 4

Advanced

4.1 How does Spark's Catalyst optimizer work under the hood?

Apache Spark's Catalyst Optimizer is one of the key components aimed at optimizing the execution performance of Spark operations. It's an optimization framework present in Spark SQL, which applies a series of transformations to a query to create an optimal execution plan.

The working of the Catalyst Optimizer can be broken down into the four phases:

1. **Analysis**: In the analysis phase, an Abstract Syntax Tree (AST) is built from the input SQL query. This tree is resolved into a logical plan by mapping the names of tables and columns, verifying the presence of named attributes in the catalog, and by applying the necessary conversions.

2. **Logical Optimization**: Once the logical plan is formed, a set of

standard optimization techniques are applied to it such as predicate pushdown, projection pruning, boolean simplification, etc. At the end of this phase, there is an optimized logical plan.

3. **Physical Planning**: The optimized logical plan then goes through the physical planning phase. The Catalyst optimizer generates multiple physical plans from the logical plan, each denoting a different strategy. It uses statistical data from its catalog and applies cost-based optimization to choose the best query execution plan.

4. **Code Generation**: The chosen physical plan is then converted into executable code. It leverages whole-stage code generation and uses 'Janino' (a runtime code compiler for Java) to compile Java bytecode, which can be directly loaded into the JVM. This significantly improves the efficiency of the execution process.

All these steps of the optimization improve the speed at which the query is processed and efficiently use system resources. It is also worth mentioning that Catalyst's rule-based optimization system allows the inclusion of new optimization techniques by adding rules, which makes it easy to extend.

For example, let's consider a Spark SQL operation:

```
spark.sql("SELECT␣a,␣b␣FROM␣table1␣WHERE␣a␣>␣5")
```

In Catalyst optimizer:

- During the Analysis phase, it would resolve the names "a", "b", and "table1".

- After analysis, it would convert it into a Logical Plan resembling 'project ["a", "b"] -> filter ["a > 5"] -> scan ["table1"]'.

- During the Logic Optimization phase, it might realize there's no need to scan "b" before the filter operation.

- In the Physical Planning phase, it would consider using different RDD operation strategies.

- During the Code Generation phase, it directly converts the chosen physical plan into the Java bytecode.

This whole process can result in quite substantial speed-ups and efficiency gains in Apache Spark jobs.

4.2 Explain the differences between cache() and persist(). How would you choose the storage level?

'cache()' and 'persist()' are two methods in Apache Spark for persisting the RDDs (Resilient Distributed Datasets) and DataFrames to speed up the computation of iterative algorithms.

'cache()' is a method that persists an RDD or DataFrame into memory. By default, 'cache()' will store the data in memory, and will spill to disk if there is not enough memory. It is actually a shortcut for using 'persist()' with the default storage level 'MEMORY_AND_DISK'. The internal implementation of 'cache()' calls 'persist()' with no arguments.

Here is an example of using 'cache()':

```
val rdd = sc.textFile("file.txt")
rdd.cache()
```

On the other hand, 'persist()' method allows you to specify the storage level. The storage level determines where the data should be stored (memory, disk, or off-heap), the replication factor (i.e., the number of copies to be stored), and whether to store the data serialized or deserialized.

Here is an example of using 'persist()' with a specific storage level:

```
import org.apache.spark.storage.StorageLevel._

val rdd = sc.textFile("file.txt")
rdd.persist(MEMORY_ONLY_SER_2)
```

In this example, 'MEMORY_ONLY_SER_2' means that the RDD

should be stored in memory, should be serialized, and two copies should be kept.

Choosing the storage level depends on your particular use-case:

- 'MEMORY_ONLY': This level will store the RDD in memory as much as possible. If the RDD does not fit in memory, some partitions will not be cached and will be recomputed on-the-fly each time they are needed.

- 'MEMORY_AND_DISK': This level will store the RDD in memory as well as on disk if it does not fit in memory.

- 'MEMORY_ONLY_SER': This level will store the RDD in serialized format thus reducing cpu/memory cost, but increasing processing time as it requires serialization/deserialization.

- 'MEMORY_AND_DISK_SER': It acts similar to 'MEMORY_ONLY_SER' and stores any RDD partitions not fitting in memory onto disk.

- 'DISK_ONLY': This level stores the RDD partitions only on disk.

- 'OFF_HEAP': This experimental option allows Spark to store the RDD in serialized format off-heap.

Here are some points to consider when choosing the storage level:

- If you have ample memory and want the fastest computation, then use 'MEMORY_ONLY'.

- If you are dealing with a lot of data that won't fit into memory, use 'MEMORY_AND_DISK' to leverage both memory and disk storage.

- If you want to minimize memory usage at the expense of CPU cycles, use the serialized formats 'MEMORY_ONLY_SER' or 'MEMORY_AND_DISK_SER'.

- If your data is computed extremely quickly, 'DISK_ONLY' could be the better choice because it doesn't use any memory.

- Use replication levels greater than 1 (like 'MEMORY_ONLY_2' or 'MEMORY_AND_DISK_2') only when you have data that is extremely expensive to compute, or when fast fault recovery is necessary.

Remember that there is a trade-off between CPU, memory, and I/O costs when picking the storage level. It is a critical decision that depends on your specific scenario and requirements.

4.3 Describe the process of shuffling in Spark and its impact on performance.

Shuffling in Apache Spark is the mechanism of redistributing the data across various partitions that might lead to data being moved across the executors and even machines. This event happens when certain operations (known as transformations), which requires the data redistribution, are invoked. Some of the transformations that cause a shuffle are 'groupByKey()', 'reduceByKey()', 'join()', 'cogroup()', 'cartesian()', etc.

During the shuffling process, all the output data from the former stages gets redistributed across partitions and can cause the data to be sent across the network to different nodes, causing a greater expense.

Let's consider a simple example:

```
val rdd = sparkContext.parallelize(List(("apple", 3), ("banana", 2), ("orange
    ", 4), ("banana", 5), ("orange", 3)), 2)
val rdd2 = rdd.reduceByKey(_ + _)
rdd2.collect
```

Here, 'sparkContext.parallelize' creates an RDD with 2 partitions. The 'reduceByKey(_ + _)' function then forces a shuffle so that all the keys of the same type are on the same partition.

Impact on performance:

1. **Network I/O:** Shuffle operations result in data being transferred over the network between executors, causing significant overhead related to network I/O.

2. **Disk I/O:** Data is written to and read from the disk during shuffle operations can be inefficient and slow.

3. **Serialization and deserialization overheads:** The data being shuffled needs to be serialized before the transfer and deserialized after the transfer, adding to the computational overhead.

4. **Partitions becoming too large or numerous:** This may lead
to a situation where individual tasks are too large and cause out of
memory errors, or when the number of individual tasks is too high,
causing non-trivial scheduling overheads.

To optimize performance during shuffle operations, you can take several measures, including:

1. Reducing the amount of data being shuffled by pre-filtering data, or
using operations like 'reduceByKey' instead of 'groupByKey'.

2. Tuning the level of parallelism during shuffle operations by controlling
the number of partitions.

3. Enabling Spark's external shuffle service to persist shuffle data and
avoid recomputation in case of a failure of an executor running shuffle
map tasks.

4. Using serialized formats that are both smaller and faster to serialize
and deserialize.

5. Ensuring you have sufficient memory to accommodate shuffled data.

4.4   How does Spark handle memory management in terms of storage and execution?

Apache Spark manages memory using custom memory management
layer (Project Tungsten) that operates on serialized binary data. It
uses off-heap memory to avoid the cost of JVM Garbage Collection
and allow it to operate on serialized data directly.

Tungsten's memory management model is designed around two main
techniques:

1. **Binary Processing**: It manages memory explicitly and eliminates the JVM object model overhead, which helps it to increase
memory scalability and reduce garbage collection costs.

2. **Cache-Aware Computation**: It leverages modern CPUs' caches to improve computation speed. It uses advanced data structures like compressed bitmaps, arrays, hash tables, sorters, etc.

Apache Spark divides the memory of each executor into two regions:

- **Execution Memory**: This memory is used for operations like shuffles, joins, sorts, and aggregations. On the execution side, memory is further divided into the shuffle, storage, and user data buffers like reduce tasks.

- **Storage Memory**: This is used for caching and propagating internal data across nodes. On the storage side, RDDs, Broadcast Variables, and other cached data are stored.

Spark provides a unified memory manager that can transparently share the memory pool between execution and storage. Spark's memory manager lets the user data structures (RDDs) borrow memory from the execution whenever they are not actively being computed, and vice versa.

Here is an example of how spark configuration for memory management looks like:

```
--executor-memory 20g
--conf spark.driver.memory=10g
--conf spark.executor.extraJavaOptions=-XX:+UseG1GC
```

In the above snippet,

- '–executor-memory 20g': This sets the total size of memory allocated for each executor.

- 'spark.driver.memory=10g': The amount of memory allocated to the driver.

- 'spark.executor.extraJavaOptions=-XX:+UseG1GC': This is used to configure the garbage collector to use.

Remember, it's always important to tune these parameters according to your dataset and resource availability. The goal of tuning the memory is to efficiently utilize the resources that are available and maximize the application's performance.

4.5   What are the challenges with using join() operations in Spark, and how can they be optimized?

Join operations in Apache Spark are essential for combining data from different DataFrames or RDDs, however, they can present a few performance-related issues:

1. **Skewness**: A skewed join happens when a few keys take a significant amount of data compared to others in the same table. This creates a scenario where some tasks take longer time to complete than others, leading to idle resources.

2. **Shuffle**: Join operations often cause shuffle, i.e., redistribution of data across multiple partitions, leading to data being serialized and transferred over the network, thus becoming a significant bottleneck.

3. **Memory usage**: Inefficient join operations can blow up the memory usage, and potentially cause out-of-memory errors.

To optimize Spark join operations, you can use the subsequent techniques:

1. **Broadcast Hash Join**: If one of your DataFrames is small enough to fit in memory, you can use a broadcast hash join, this sends a copy of the small DataFrame to all nodes, therefore removing the need for reshuffling during the join. This can significantly speed up the join process.

```
from pyspark.sql.functions import broadcast
largeDF.join(broadcast(smallDF), "id")
```

2. **Bucketing**: Bucketing is a technique in which you can specify the number of buckets you want to divide your data. Data is parti-

tioned according to the hash of the join key, this technique can reduce shuffle when joining on the bucketed key.

```
df.write.bucketBy(100, "id").sortBy("id").saveAsTable("people_bucketed")
```

3. **Salting**: Salting is a technique for dealing with skewed data. It involves adding a random number (the salt) to each key on both DataFrames, this spreads the records of popular keys evenly across multiple partitions.

```
from pyspark.sql.functions import rand

df1.withColumn("salt", (rand()*10).cast("int")).join(df2.withColumn("salt", (
    rand()*10).cast("int")), ["id", "salt"])
```

4. **Avoid Cartesian Products**: A Cartesian product join creates a combination of all rows which can cause the number of records to explode, you should always specify the join column(s) to prevent this from happening. If you have to perform a cross join, ensure your data is sufficiently small.

It's also important to monitor your Spark Application UI to understand the performance impact of your join operations and adjust the strategies appropriately.

4.6 Explain the concept of "watermarking" in Spark Streaming.

Watermarking in Spark Streaming is a mechanism to limit the input data that needs to be processed by Spark Streaming applications. This mechanism is primarily used in the context of event time-based processing and window operations.

When dealing with a stream of data, events can get delayed and arrive out of order due to various reasons such as network issues or disparities in the event generation time. As a result, the application needs to delay processing to handle such late arrivals, which maintains state and data for longer times, causing more resource consumption. So, there needs to be a limit on how late the data can be, and that is where watermarking comes into play.

A watermark is a threshold that tells the system that there will be no more data with event time earlier than this threshold. It is used to denote the progress of event time in data stream processing. When you define a watermark for your data, it allows the system to assume that no data older than the watermark will be seen in future.

Let's take an example. If the current watermark is "12:00", it indicates that no event time earlier than "12:00" will be seen in the stream. So, any window operation on the stream will not consider any event with event times earlier than this watermark.

You can define watermark in Spark Streaming using the 'withWatermark' function like this:

```
inputDF
  .withWatermark("eventTime", "10 minutes") // Using event time watermarking
  .groupBy(
    window($"eventTime", "10 minutes", "5 minutes"), $"userId")
  .count()
```

In this example, 'eventTime' refers to the time column in your DataFrame and '10 minutes' is the delay threshold. It indicates that the system won't expect any data older than 10 minutes w.r.t. to the latest data that it has seen.

By using watermarking, you effectively limit the amount of intermediate state that needs to be kept for processing each window slice. Spark will automatically clear old state once it's no longer required, mitigating the risk of your system running out of memory during the processing of large streams.

4.7 How does Spark's Tungsten engine improve performance?

Project Tungsten, implemented in Apache Spark from version 1.4, focuses on improving Spark's performance in data processing. It achieves this by leveraging the principles of modern compilers and various hardware capabilities like CPU registers and cache hierarchies. Below are some main performance enhancements provided by Tungsten:

1. **Memory Management:** Traditional Java objects can have considerable overhead due to object headers, object alignment, and reference fields. Tungsten provides a binary format to manage memory explicitly and eliminates Java object overhead. This allows Spark to store more data in memory.

2. **Cache Locality:** Tungsten optimizes the layout of data in memory to exploit CPU cache, which significantly speeds up data processing tasks by reducing the cache miss rate.

3. **Code Generation:** Tungsten includes a compiler that can generate bytecode to implement queries, which allows it to exploit modern CPUs' pipelining abilities and avoid unnecessary interpretation overhead.

Here is an example of how Spark SQL generates Java code at runtime:

```
public Object generate(Object[] references) {
    return new GeneratedIterator(references);
}

class GeneratedIterator extends org.apache.spark.sql.execution.
    BufferedRowIterator {
    ...
    // code for processing each row of each batch
}
```

4. **Operator Fusion:** Tungsten utilizes a technique known as "whole-stage code generation" that allows it to fuse multiple operations together into a single function, to avoid the overhead of function calls and to enable further compiler optimizations.

5. **Off-heap Memory:** In regular JVM heap memory, garbage collection can degrade the performance of Spark applications. Tungsten avoids this overhead by maintaining data off-heap.

The Tungsten project has significantly improved the efficiency of Spark applications, especially those involving large data volumes, allowing Spark to better compete with engines written in lower-level languages like C++.

4.8   Describe the differences between DataFrame, Dataset, and RDD. When would you prefer one over the others?

The three primary data structures in Apache Spark are RDDs (Resilient Distributed Datasets), DataFrames, and Datasets. Each has its own advantages and use cases.

1. RDD (Resilient Distributed Datasets)

RDD is the fundamental data structure of Spark and it is an immutable distributed collection of objects. Each dataset in RDD is divided into logical partitions, which may be computed on different nodes of the cluster.

Pros:

  - Supports any data type that can be serialized by Java

  - Provides low level functionality and high-level abstractions

  - Usage of transformations and actions to perform computations on data

  - Failure recovery handled by Spark via RDD lineage graph

Cons:

  - Computations on RDDs do not fully use Spark's optimizations

- Does not reveal what the data is, such as the datatype of columns, column names, etc.

2. DataFrame

DataFrame is an untyped distributed collection of data. Therefore, the schema of DataFrame is not checked at compile time but only at runtime, when the query is run. DataFrame only keeps column names and data types, including binary data.

Pros:

- Allows developers to impose a structure onto it in a form of a pre-defined schema

- Great performance optimization due to Tungsten and Catalyst

- Can be integrated with various data formats (like JSON, Hive, and parquet) and storage systems (like HDFS, HBase, MySQL, etc.)

Cons: - User gets no compile-time type safety

3. Dataset

A Dataset is a distributed collection of data which provides the benefits of RDDs (strong typing, ability to use functional programming operations) with the benefits of the Spark DataFrame's optimized execution engine. You get a unified programming interface, high-level abstraction, and native optimization.

Pros:

- Encoders for most common types are automatically created

- Enables powerful interactive and programmatic features.

- Type-safe, object-oriented programming style

Cons: - Less efficient than DataFrames for operations that don't benefit from type safety

To decide when to use which, it's important to understand the nature and requirements of your task:

- If you require fine-grained control over your data and operations, use RDDs.

- If you need a general, powerful, and high-level abstraction tool, use DataFrames.

- If you require the benefits of RDDs with the optimization techniques and power of DataFrames, go for Datasets.

4.9   How can you optimize a Spark application for running on a cluster with limited resources?

Efficiently running a Spark application on a limited-resources cluster requires careful resource management and optimizing the Spark application's configuration settings. Here are a few strategies to consider:

1. **Sizing of Executors**: Executors are the working units of Spark. Set the number of cores and heap size to make it fit in your cluster. You should avoid network I/O by minimizing shuffling and avoiding operations like 'groupByKey()'. Instead, use operations like 'reduceByKey()' which reduce data locally.

```
spark = SparkSession.builder
.master("local")
.appName("Word Count")
.config("spark.executor.memory", "1gb")
.getOrCreate()
```

In the above configuration, 'spark.executor.memory' is being set to '1gb'.

2. **Caching/Persistence**: Use 'cache()' or 'persist()' to keep the frequently accessed or reused RDDs into memory for faster access. But do this judiciously as it can consume a lot of memory.

```
rdd = sc.parallelize(data)
rdd.cache()
```

This will store the RDD 'rdd' in memory.

3. **Adjusting the Level of Parallelism**: Too few partitions can limit parallelism since only one task can be computed per partition simultaneously. However, too many partitions can also slow down your program because scheduling a task in Spark has some overhead. Generally, 2-3 tasks per CPU core in your cluster are recommended.

```
rdd = sc.parallelize(data, 10) # Creating 10 partitions
```

In the above configuration, 'numPartitions' is set to '10'.

4. **Serialization**: Use Serialization to speed up the task sending over the network or writing to Disk. Kryo serialization is more compact and faster than Java serialization. Also, serialized RDDs can be stored more compactly in memory.

```
spark = SparkSession.builder
.master("local")
.appName("Word Count")
.config("spark.serializer", "org.apache.spark.serializer.KryoSerializer")
.getOrCreate()
```

In the above configuration, 'spark.serializer' is set to 'org.apache.spark.serializer.KryoSerializer'.

5. **Broadcast Variables**: If your application needs to send a large read-only lookup table to all the executor nodes, use Broadcast Variables. These variables are cached on each machine, and not sent over the network with each stage.

```
broadcastVar = sc.broadcast([1, 2, 3])
```

The above code creates a broadcast variable 'broadcastVar'.

By implementing these strategies, you can optimize a Spark application for running on a cluster with limited resources.

4.10 What are the potential issues with using broadcast variables in a Spark application?

Broadcast variables in Apache Spark are read-only shared variables that are cached and available on each machine rather than sending a copy of the variable with tasks. They are used to give nodes access to a large input dataset in an efficient manner.

Even though broad variables can optimize the performance of your Spark application, there are certain issues that you might encounter when using them:

1. **Memory Consumption:** Broadcast variables are stored in the memory of each worker node. If the data is too big, it could consume a significant amount of memory in the worker nodes leading to out of memory errors. It's important to ensure that your worker nodes have enough memory.

```
# Broadcasting a large variable
large_variable = range(1000000)
bc_large_variable = spark.sparkContext.broadcast(large_variable)
```

2. **Serialization:** The data that will be broadcasted needs to be serializable. Non-serializable objects cannot be broadcasted. This can cause issues when attempting to broadcast complex objects. You need to ensure that the data can be serialized and deserialized accurately.

3. **Immutability:** Broadcast variables are read-only which means they can't be changed once they are defined. This could be less flexible if your application requires updating the variables.

```
# Trying to update a broadcast variable
bc_variable = spark.sparkContext.broadcast([1, 2, 3, 4, 5])
bc_variable.value.append(6) # this line throws an error because broadcast
    variables are read-only
```

4. **Cached Forever:** Once a variable is broadcasted, it remains in the memory and doesn't get deleted. If there are a large number

of broadcast variables that are no longer necessary, they consume memory unnecessarily.

In conclusion, while using broadcast variables in Spark applications can greatly improve performance by reducing data transfer, care must be taken to manage memory usage, ensure data is serializable, and remember that once broadcast, the variables are read-only and remain in memory till your application runs.

4.11 How does Spark ensure data integrity and fault tolerance in Spark Streaming applications?

Apache Spark ensures data integrity and fault tolerance in Spark Streaming applications via several mechanisms including RDD checkpointing, Write Ahead Logs (WALs), storing RDDs in memory with replication, and tracking RDD lineage.

1. RDD Checkpointing: Checkpointing is the process of saving the generated Resilient Distributed Datasets (RDDs) to a reliable storage system (like HDFS). The checkpointed RDDs cut the lineage of RDD computations, thereby reducing the cost of failure recovery. For example,

```
StreamingContext ssc = new StreamingContext(sparkConf, batchInterval);
ssc.checkpoint(checkpointDirectory);
```

This makes sure that the metadata of the DStream (not the actual data) and the RDDs (generated by the DStream) are periodically check-pointed to a reliable storage system like HDFS.

2. Write Ahead Logs (WALs): Spark Streaming also provides a Write Ahead Logs (WAL) feature. WALs log the input data received by Spark Streaming before processing it. So, if there is a failure, the system can recover the data from the logs. You can enable this with:

```
sparkConf.set("spark.streaming.receiver.writeAheadLog.enable", "true");
```

3. In-Memory with Replication: RDDs can be stored in memory with multiple replicas across the worker nodes. This helps in quick regeneration of lost data due to node failures.

4. Tracking RDD Lineage: Spark Streaming uses the lineage information of RDDs (i.e., the series of transformations that produced an RDD) to rebuild lost data. For example, if the lineage of an RDD shows it was mapped from another RDD with a function 'f', Spark will reapply 'f' to the input data to regenerate the RDD.

It's important to note that fault tolerance techniques have an impact on the resources and performance of the Spark Streaming application. Enabling checkpointing and WALs, and storing RDDs with replication involves additional I/O operations, storage requirements and recovery time, which can impact the overall performance of the application.

Nonetheless, these mechanisms ensure the integrity of data and result in a robust streaming application capable of recovering from failures.

4.12   Explain the role and working of the DAG scheduler in Spark.

The Directed Acyclic Graph (DAG) Scheduler in Apache Spark is the scheduling layer of Apache Spark that is responsible for converting a physical execution plan (i.e., an RDD lineage graph) into stages of tasks that get executed on a cluster.

Let's break it down a bit to understand better:

- **Spark DAG**: When you create Spark transformations on RDD (like map, flatmap etc.), Spark creates a logical execution plan. This plan, visualized as a graph where nodes are RDD partitions and edges are the transformations applied on those partitions, is what's called a Directed Acyclic Graph.

- **Scheduler**: The Scheduler's role is to take this graph and translate it into physical execution units, grouping transformations into stages - sequences of transformations which can be executed together in a single step without exchanging data over the network.

- **Stages**: Stages are created by breaking the graph at points where data needs to be redistributed, these transformations are called "shuffle dependencies". Tasks within a single stage don't have shuffle dependencies between them, and can be computed in no particular order, often in parallel.

- **Tasks**: Each stage is divided into tasks. A task is the smallest unit of work sent to an executor, computation to be performed over an RDD partition.

- **Working of DAG Scheduler**: When an action is called on the RDD, Spark creates the DAG and submits it to the DAG scheduler. The DAGScheduler divides operators into stages of tasks. A stage is comprised of tasks based on their dependencies on some dataset. All tasks in a particular stage can be executed in parallel. The DAGScheduler pipelines operators together. For example, many map operators can be scheduled in a single stage. The final result of a DAG scheduler is a set of stages. The stages are submitted to the TaskScheduler. The TaskScheduler launches tasks via cluster manager (Spark Standalone/Yarn/Mesos).

Here is a simplistic example:

```
val data = spark.textFile("some_text.txt")
val mapped = data.map(line => line.split(" ").size)
val reduced = mapped.reduce((a, b) => if (a > b) a else b)
```

- You read a text file ('data'), this is your input RDD, it has partitions depending on the number of blocks of the files.

- Map operation is defined on 'data', producing a transformation.

- Reduce operation is defined on 'result' of map operation, causing shuffle dependency.

This creates a two-stage DAG: the map operations can be executed together in a first stage, and they are followed by a reduce operation in a second stage. DAGScheduler will then schedule tasks following this stage structure.

4.13   How do you handle late-arriving data in Spark Streaming?

In Spark Streaming, late-arriving data refers to data that arrives after the window for which it was intended. Depending on the processing requirements of the stream, this data can be handled using Spark Streaming's built-in support for late data, or via custom processing logic.

One way to handle late-arriving data is with Apache Spark's 'updateStateByKey' operation. This operation provides you with a state (data) and a sequence of new values (updates). The operation applies these updates to the state on a per-key basis, updating the value for a key based on the new data. This provides a way to continually update the state with new data as it arrives, regardless of whether the data is late-arriving.

Here is a simple example of how you could use 'updateStateByKey' to handle late-arriving data:

```
val updateFunc = (values: Seq[Int], state: Option[Int]) => {
  val currentCount = values.sum
  val previousCount = state.getOrElse(0)
  Some(currentCount + previousCount)
}

val stateDstream = pairs.updateStateByKey[Int](updateFunc)
```

In this example, 'values' represents the new values for a key, and 'state' represents the current state of the key. The 'updateFunc' function updates the state by adding the sum of the new values to the previous state.

Late-arriving data could also be handled using windowed computations along with the 'reduceByKeyAndWindow' function. In this
case, you can define a window of time, and apply a reduction function over that window. This function retains data for a longer period
before performing the calculation, allowing for late-arriving data to
still be accounted for.

For instance:

```
val windowedWordCounts = pairs
  .reduceByKeyAndWindow((a:Int,b:Int) => (a + b), Minutes(10), Seconds(2))
```

Here, data is aggregated over the last 10 minutes of data, and the
window is slid every 2 seconds, allowing for late data within the 10
minutes window.

Always remember, dealing with late-arriving data often involves making a tradeoff between accuracy and latency. If you need high accuracy, you may need to accommodate late-arriving data which can
increase latency. If low latency is more important, you may need to
process data as it arrives and tolerate a certain level of inaccuracies.

4.14 Describe the process of dynamic re-source allocation in Spark.

Dynamic Resource Allocation is a feature in Apache Spark that lets
your Spark application release resources it is not using and acquire
resources that it can use. This can be particularly helpful when your
application has stages with varying resource requirements or you have
several concurrently running applications.

When dynamic allocation is enabled, a Spark application initially
starts with a small number of executors. As the application progresses, it requests additional executors as necessary (based on task
backlog) and releases executors that have been idle for an extended
period of time.

Here is an overview of the entire process:

1. **Starting with a small number of executors:** When a Spark application is submitted, it is initially allocated with a small number of executors.

2. **Requesting additional executors:** When there are pending tasks in a Spark application's scheduler queue, the application can request additional executors from the cluster manager. The scaling up factor is controlled by 'spark.dynamicAllocation.schedulerBacklogTimeout'.

3. **Allocating new executors:** Once the request is sent to the cluster manager for additional executors, the cluster manager attempts to allocate as many new executor processes as it can, given the availability of resources in the cluster.

4. **Releasing idle executors:** If an executor has been idle for a long time, the application can also give these resources back to the cluster manager, so other applications could potentially use them. The idle time is controlled by 'spark.dynamicAllocation.executorIdleTimeout'.

5. **Effect of caching on executor release:** If an executor has cached blocks of data, these blocks are not removed unless the executor has been idle for a significant amount of time ('spark.dynamicAllocation.cachedExecutorIdleTimeout').

You can enable dynamic resource allocation by setting 'spark.dynamicAllocation.enabled' to 'true' in 'spark.conf'. Note that external shuffle service must be enabled if you use dynamic allocation.

Here are some key parameters to tweak the behavior of Dynamic Resource Allocation:

- 'spark.dynamicAllocation.initialExecutors': Initial number of executors to run if dynamic allocation is enabled.

- 'spark.dynamicAllocation.minExecutors': Lower bound for the number of executors if dynamic allocation is enabled.

- 'spark.dynamicAllocation.maxExecutors': Upper bound for the number of executors if dynamic allocation is enabled.

- 'spark.dynamicAllocation.schedulerBacklogTimeout': Number of seconds that a Spark application waits, if there are pending tasks in the application's scheduler queue, before requesting more executors.

- 'spark.dynamicAllocation.executorIdleTimeout': If an executor runs no tasks for this duration, it will be removed.

- 'spark.dynamicAllocation.cachedExecutorIdleTimeout': If an executor (with cached blocks) runs no tasks for this duration, it will be removed.

Here is a sample configuration:

```
spark = SparkSession.builder
    .appName("Spark Dynamic Allocation")
    .config("spark.dynamicAllocation.enabled", "true")
    .config("spark.shuffle.service.enabled", "true")
    .config("spark.dynamicAllocation.minExecutors", "1")
    .config("spark.dynamicAllocation.maxExecutors", "100")
    .config("spark.dynamicAllocation.initialExecutors", "10")
    .getOrCreate()
```

In this example, dynamic allocation is enabled with a minimum of 1 executor and a maximum of 100 executors. There are initially 10 executors. The application will request more or release some depending on its needs. It's worth mentioning that dynamic allocation works in tandem with the external shuffle service hence 'spark.shuffle.service.enabled' is set to true.

4.15 How can you monitor and debug performance issues in a Spark application?

Monitoring and debugging performance problems in a Spark application involve the following methods:

1. **Spark Application UI:** The Spark Application UI provides a wealth of information to help understand the performance of Spark jobs. It provides metrics about tasks, durations, sizes of data read/written, and many more. You can access it by simply opening the

URL http://<driver-node>:4040 in a web browser, or through the
link provided in the Spark shell.

Let's say you have a job that seems to be running slower than you'd
expect. You might start by checking:

(a) The timeline view of the stages page:

```
<img width="640" src="https://spark.apache.org/docs/latest/img/webui-
    stagespage.png">
```

This gives an overview of how time is being spent. If you see a lot of
red area, that can indicate time being spent on garbage collection.

(b) Summary metrics for stages:

```
<img width="640" src="https://spark.apache.org/docs/latest/img/webui-
    stagespage-summary.png">
```

This can be useful to see if there is skew in the size of tasks that
could be slowing the job down, or if a lot of time is being spent on
serialization or getting data from HDFS.

2. **Spark logs:** Spark logs also provide critical information about
the application, such as Spark environment settings, stages and tasks
information, job start, and end-times, etc. They can be set to different
levels – such as INFO, DEBUG, WARN, and ERROR – to control
the verbosity.

For example, to set the log level to WARN:

```
val sc: SparkContext = ...
sc.setLogLevel("WARN")
```

3. **Metrics System:** Spark provides a metrics system based on
the Dropwizard Metrics Library to collect metrics about the behavior of various Spark components. This can be extremely useful for
understanding how Spark is using resources. The metrics system can
be configured separately for the driver and each executor in the cluster, it also supports a variety of sinks like Console, CSV, Ganglia,
Graphite, etc.

Here is a configuration example:

```
spark.metrics.namespace=MySparkApp
spark.metrics.conf.*.sink.console.class=org.apache.spark.metrics.sink.
    ConsoleSink
spark.metrics.conf.*.sink.console.period=1
spark.metrics.conf.*.sink.console.unit=minutes
spark.metrics.conf.master.source.master.class=org.apache.spark.metrics.source.
    MasterSource
spark.metrics.conf.worker.source.worker.class=org.apache.spark.metrics.source.
    WorkerSource
```

4. **Profiling:** You can also use a profiler like YourKit, which provides a JVM profiler tool to identify performance bottlenecks in Spark applications. The MicroStrategy Spark Profiler is a tool that helps you understand how time and resources such as CPU and memory are consumed by Spark apps.

5. **SparkListeners:** Apache Spark provides APIs to plug in your own custom listeners, which handle events from Spark's execution engine, such as job completion and executor failure. These listeners can be used to track progress and debug problems programmatically.

For example, the following listener logs the time spent on each stage:

```
class MySparkListener extends SparkListener {
  override def onStageCompleted(stageCompleted: StageCompleted) {
    val duration = stageCompleted.stageInfo.completionTime.get -
      stageCompleted.stageInfo.submissionTime.get
    println(s"Stage ${stageCompleted.stageInfo.stageId} took ${duration} ms")
  }
}
val conf: SparkConf = new SparkConf().setAppName("My app").setMaster("local")
val sc: SparkContext = new SparkContext(conf)
sc.addSparkListener(new MySparkListener)
```

All these techniques will give you valuable insights into your Spark applications and help you understand where and why performance problems are occurring.

4.16   What is off-heap memory in Spark, and when would you use it?

Off-heap memory in Apache Spark refers to the memory space that resides outside the main memory heap that is managed by the JVM (Java Virtual Machine). By not being part of the JVM heap, off-heap memory can help to overcome certain limitations associated with Java garbage collection, which can have performance impacts on the Spark application.

To elaborate, the JVM's Garbage Collection (GC) can affect the performance of Spark applications in two ways. First, because garbage collection is an automatic process, it can cause unpredictable delays as it cleans up unused objects from memory. Larger heaps may result in longer garbage collection pauses. Second, a large JVM heap size can decrease the efficiency of memory use due to safe points issues (when JVM briefly pauses all application threads).

Off-heap memory can alleviate some of these issues. Since off-heap data is not subject to Java's garbage collection, you can store large datasets in off-heap memory without incurring the performance cost of frequent or prolonged GC pauses. Moreover, off-heap memory allows Spark to interact with other libraries or frameworks that also make use of off-heap storage, like Apache Arrow or external databases.

However, using off-heap memory necessitates manual memory management, which can complicate your code.

In Spark, to use off-heap memory, we're required to set a couple configurations:

```
spark.memory.offHeap.enabled true
spark.memory.offHeap.size <size_in_bytes>
```

Here, 'spark.memory.offHeap.size' defines the total amount of memory, in bytes, that can be allocated for off-heap storage.

It's worth noting that the exact circumstances under which off-heap memory offers a performance advantage can depend on the specific demands and constraints of your application. So, as a rule of thumb, it's best to understand the characteristics of your Spark application, and monitor its performance with (and without) off-heap memory before deciding to use this feature.

4.17 Explain the differences between window, groupby, and reduceby operations in Spark Streaming.

In Apache Spark, window, groupBy and reduceByKey operations play a significant role in transforming the data. They provide ways to manipulate distributed datasets for different types of computations.

1. Window operations:

Window operations allow you to apply transformations over a sliding window of data in the DStream. Every time the window slides over the DStream, the source DStream's RDDs that fall within the window are combined and operated upon to produce the RDDs of the windowed DStream. It takes two parameters - window length and sliding interval.

windowedWordCounts = pairs.window(Seconds(30), Seconds(10))

In the above example, the window length is 30 seconds and sliding interval is 10 seconds, meaning it will consider last 30 seconds of data and move the window every 10 seconds.

2. GroupBy operations:

GroupBy operations are basically transforming the data in such a way that it groups the elements of the source dataset. This operation returns a new RDD that has key-value pairs where the key is the grouped data and value is the iterable of all values with the same key.

```
rdd = sc.parallelize([("a", 1), ("b", 1), ("a", 1)])
grouped = rdd.groupByKey()
for key, values in grouped.collect():
    print(key, list(values))
```

In the above example, the key is the first letter of each tuple and the output will be ('a', [1, 1]), ('b', [1]).

3. ReduceByKey operations:

ReduceByKey operations are transformations that reduce values with the same key using some function. These operations are beneficial because they can combine output with a common key on the same worker node before shuffling the data.

```
rdd = sc.parallelize([("a", 1), ("b", 1), ("a", 1)])
reduced = rdd.reduceByKey(lambda a, b: a+b)
print(reduced.collect())
```

In the last example, the output will be: [('a', 2), ('b', 1)]. For each key, it is aggregating (summing) its values.

The main differences are:

- GroupBy forms pairs of data and grouping keys, which does not require combining output with a common key at each partition before shuffling the data, and it needn't split resulting data.

- ReduceByKey operates locally on each partition, thus reducing data shuffling over the network.

- Window operations perform transformations on batches of data. Operations are performed on a sliding window of data in DStream, providing more flexible time sensitive analysis.

4.18 How do you handle data serialization in Spark to optimize performance?

Apache Spark supports two serialization libraries:

1. Java serialization: By default, Spark serializes objects using Java's ObjectOutputStream framework which can work with any class that implements java.io.Serializable. This serialization method is flexible but often quite slow and ends up producing large serialized formats.

2. Kryo serialization: Spark can also use the Kryo library to serialize objects. Kryo has a more compact serialized format and is often faster than Java serialization, but it does not support all serializable types and requires to register custom classes in advance for the best performance.

To extend, you can switch to Kryo by setting SparkConf in your application like below:

```
val conf = new SparkConf().setAppName("MyApp")
conf.set("spark.serializer", "org.apache.spark.serializer.KryoSerializer")
```

And for registering custom classes:

```
conf.registerKryoClasses(Array(classOf[MyCustomClass], classOf[
    AnotherCustomClass]))
```

Another way to optimize performance when transmitting data over the network during shuffle operations, you can enable the serialized RDD compression while shuffling by setting the 'spark.shuffle.compress' to true.

```
conf.set("spark.shuffle.compress", "true")
```

Also, when data is stored persistently in serialized form, Apache Spark can save substantial space by compressing that data. You can select a codec with the 'spark.io.compression.codec' configuration. The default codec is 'lz4' but you can change it to others like 'lzf', 'snappy', etc.

```
conf.set("spark.io.compression.codec", "lz4")
```

This type of tunings mainly depends on your dataset and the nature of your operations. There isn't a one-size-fits-all codec, so you should pick the right compression codec according to your needs. Remember to consider both the CPU and the I/O this saves.

4.19 Describe the benefits and challenges of using Spark with Kubernetes.

Using Apache Spark along with Kubernetes brings in a host of advantages and few challenges as well. Let's delve into each one of them:

Benefits:

1. **Scaling**: Kubernetes provides easy, out-of-the-box, fault-tolerant, scalable cluster management. With Kubernetes, you can start with a small amount of nodes for your Spark applications and scale up as your workload increases.

2. **Resource Management**: Kubernetes eliminates the need for a separate resource manager like YARN or Mesos, thereby simplifying your architecture. With Kubernetes, you can specify the amount of CPU and memory that each Spark executor should have, and Kubernetes will ensure that the resources are available.

3. **Portability**: Kubernetes can run on a variety of platforms, whether on-premise or in the Cloud, so your Spark applications can be written once and run anywhere.

4. **Isolation**: Kubernetes allows each Spark application to have its own isolated environment with its own resources, dependencies, configurations etc.

5. **Deployment Flexibility**: It's easier with Kubernetes to deploy

Spark in different environments - Cloud, multi-cloud, on-premises, hybrid etc.

Challenges:

1. **Learning Curve and Complex Configuration**: Kubernetes itself is a complex system with a wide variety of configuration options. Understanding these options and how they interact can be a tall order, especially for those new to the Kubernetes ecosystem.

2. **Networking Configuration**: Networking in Kubernetes is another complex aspect that needs to be handled. Network policies and security need to be established to ensure secure and efficient communication between the Spark components.

3. **Monitoring and Debugging**: Monitoring Spark applications running on Kubernetes can be more complex compared to traditional Spark cluster manager like YARN, in terms of accessing logs and profiling etc.

4. **Persistent Storage**: If persistent storage is not well managed, it could become a challenge. Kubernetes does have Persistent Volumes and Persistent Volume Claims, but their usage and handling require a good understanding of Kubernetes storage concepts.

Here's a simple example of how we can use Spark with Kubernetes:

```
bin/spark-submit
    --master k8s://https://<k8s-apiserver-host>:<k8s-apiserver-port>
    --deploy-mode cluster
    --name spark-pi
    --class org.apache.spark.examples.SparkPi
    --conf spark.executor.instances=5
    --conf spark.kubernetes.container.image=<spark-image>
    local:///opt/spark/examples/jars/spark-examples_2.12-3.1.1.jar
```

In this example, we are submitting a Spark job to a Kubernetes cluster. The Spark job is a simple "pi" calculation program. The 'spark-submit' command includes specifications for the Kubernetes master URL, the deployment mode, job name, and job class. We are specifying that we want 5 executors, and the Docker image to use for the Spark containers. With this, Kubernetes will create pods with Spark applications and orchestrate their lifecycle.

4.20 How do you ensure data consistency in Spark when integrating with external databases or data sources?

To ensure data consistency in Spark when interacting with external databases or data sources, especially in a multi-user environment, Apache Spark uses the concept of DataFrames and SparkSQL along with transactions.

Let's consider a situation where we have multiple Spark jobs reading from and writing to the same external data source. If these jobs are not properly managed, data inconsistency can occur due to concurrent read/write operations.

Here are a few strategies to ensure data consistency:

1. **Use Transactions**:

Some databases support transactions which can be used to ensure data consistency when multiple jobs are trying to access and modify the same data. This is usually done by locking the data, performing the operations, and then releasing the lock. However, transactions are expensive and can slow down the whole process if not managed properly.

```
database.transaction do
  spark.read.format("jdbc")
    .option("url", connectionUrl)
    .option("dbtable", "table")
    .option("user", user)
    .option("password", password)
    .load()
end
```

2. **Use Append Only Logs**:

This will ensure that every process (or transformation) will only be appending data to the dataset and not modifying it. It's the preferred way to go with large datasets where transactions can be very expensive or impossible.

```
dataframe.write.format("log").save("/path/to/log")
```

3. **Use Checkpoints**:

In Spark, checkpoints can help in truncating the lineage graph and they are useful for recovering from failures. Besides, they write the entire dataset to a persistent storage.

```
df.rdd.checkpoint()
```

4. **Use Write-Ahead Logs (WAL)**:

In Spark Streaming, to provide data consistency, it provides a mechanism of Write-Ahead Logs (WAL). This ensures that all the received data is saved to the log file on a distributed file system before it is processed. So even if the system fails, it can be recovered.

```
ssc = StreamingContext(sparkConf, batchInterval)
ssc.checkpoint(checkpointDirectory) # set checkpoint directory
ssc.remember(Minutes(1)) # set the remember duration
```

5. **Immutable Datasets**:

DataFrames and RDDs in Spark are immutable i.e., any transformations on these datasets will create a new dataset instead of modifying the existing one. This ensures that one job cannot affect the data being read by another job.

So the methods above can be used to ensure data consistency in Spark when integrating with external databases or data sources. However, monitoring the data consistency and handling data inconsistency when it occurs, should be a part of the data pipeline's design.

Chapter 5

Expert

5.1 Dive deep into Spark's internal execution model. How does it manage task scheduling and execution on clusters?

Apache Spark is a data processing framework that can quickly perform processing tasks on very large data sets, and can also distribute data processing tasks across multiple computers, either on its own or in tandem with other distributed computing tools.

The execution model of Spark is the core of understanding the working mechanism of Spark and essential for optimizing Spark applications.

1. **Spark Application:**

Every Spark application will have a driver program, which runs the user's 'main' function and is responsible for three key functions: maintaining information about the Spark application; responding to a user's program or input; and analyzing, distributing, and scheduling work across the executors.

2. **Spark Cluster, Executors, and Tasks:**

The executing program is divided into a set of tasks, Spark will schedule tasks on the executor, the executor is a JVM process, which actually runs tasks on a slave node. In an ideal case, each CPU core will run one task at a time (subject to available resources).

```
val rdd = sc.parallelize(1 to 100)
val rdd2 = rdd.map(x => x + 10)
rdd2.count()
```

In the code above, 'map' in 'rdd2' is a transformation, but the transformation doesn't do the compute immediately until an action is called (in this case, 'count'). When performing an action, the driver program will create tasks, then the tasks will be distributed to executors.

3. **Stages of Tasks:**

Tasks are organized into a sequence of stages. Stages can run in parallel, but tasks within a stage must run in order and only after the previous task has been completed, similar to a MapReduce job. Stages are classified into two types: ShuffleMapStages and ResultStages, separated by shuffle boundaries.

4. **Spark Scheduling:**

Scheduling in Apache Spark is based on the concept of stages. The DAGScheduler computes a DAG of stages for each job, where each stage contains tasks based on a common shuffle dependency. It also schedules these tasks via TaskScheduler and submits each task to an executor.

TaskScheduler further divides into two types: FIFO Scheduler and Fair Scheduler. FIFO schedules tasks on a first-come, first-served basis. Fair scheduling allows Spark to share resources fairly across multiple jobs.

5. **Caching and Persistence:**

Spark also provides functionalities for storing the intermediate data from different stages in memory or disk. Caching or persistence is a mechanism to speed up those computations that are reused across stages.

All of these procedures are to optimize performance in scheduling and executing tasks in a distributed manner across the cluster.

5.2 How does Spark's "adaptive query execution" (AQE) work, and what are its benefits?

Adaptive Query Execution (AQE) is a feature in Spark SQL that makes use of runtime statistics to choose the most optimal query execution plan. It introduces several optimizations at the runtime, which can lead to significant improvements in query performance.

Here is how AQE works:

1. **Dynamic Coalescing of Shuffle Partitions**: Instead of using a fixed number of shuffle partitions, Spark dynamically coalesces shuffle partitions at runtime to avoid reading small blocks and reduce the number of output partitions. This will reduce the overhead of scheduling and executing many small tasks in cases when the data is skewed or filtered heavily.

```
// Enable AQE and configure min shuffle partition number
spark.conf.set("spark.sql.adaptive.enabled", "true")
spark.conf.set("spark.sql.adaptive.coalescePartitions.minPartitionNum", "1")
```

2. **Switching Join Strategies**: At runtime, Spark can switch between broadcast hash join and sort merge join based on the actual size of input data. This is more optimal than the static strategy determined by 'spark.sql.autoBroadcastJoinThreshold'.

3. **Optimizing Skew Joins**: AQE handles skew in sort-merge join by splitting (and replicating if needed) skewed tasks into smaller tasks that can be executed in parallel.

```
// Enable skew join optimization
spark.conf.set("spark.sql.adaptive.skewJoin.enabled", "true")
spark.conf.set("spark.sql.adaptive.skewJoin.skewedPartitionFactor", "5")
```

4. **Re-optimizing Subquery**: AQE optimizes and plans the sub-query by propagating the filters from the main query.

In summary, the benefits of AQE are:

- It can dynamically adjust the number of shuffle partitions based on the data size, which can significantly improve the performance of shuffle operations.

- It adjusts the join strategies based on the actual size of the join inputs, which can avoid issues where a broadcast hash join runs out of memory because the table size is underestimated.

- It can handle skew in sort-merge join, which was a very common but difficult to deal with the issue before.

- It improves performance by re-optimizing the subquery.

Overall, AQE enhances Spark's capability to handle a variety of data and workload characteristics by leveraging runtime statistics to make more informed decisions. This allows Spark to be highly adaptive and optimize tasks dynamically, resulting in significant improvement in query execution performance.

5.3 Describe the architecture and flow of a Spark Structured Streaming application.

Apache Spark Structured Streaming is a scalable and fault-tolerant stream processing engine built on the Spark SQL engine. It allows you to express your streaming computation the same way as you would express a batch computation on static data.

The architecture of a Spark Structured Streaming application involves the following stages:

1. **Input Sources**: The data is ingressed via sources like Kafka, Flume, Kinesis, or TCP sockets, and DataFrame/Dataset APIs are used to read this data.

2. **Streaming Queries**: Queries on streaming data are expressed on the same DataFrame/Dataset APIs which transform static (batch) data.

3. **Query Execution**: The Spark SQL engine runs these queries incrementally and continuously updates the final result as streaming data continues to arrive.

4. **Output Sinks**: The result of the query (which is updated in as real-time as possible) is written out to an Output Sink like file systems, databases, dashboards, etc.

So, the basic data flow from the input source towards the output sink(s) involves the following steps:

- **Step 1**: Stream Input Source produces a stream of data which is the input data for our streaming application.

```
lines = spark.readStream.format('socket').option('host', 'localhost').option
    ('port', 9999).load()
```

- **Step 2**: The Streaming Module of Spark then divides this input data into small batches.

- **Step 3**: The small batches of input data are then processed by the Spark engine to generate the final result.

```
words = lines.select(explode(split(lines.value, ' ')).alias('word'))
wordCounts = words.groupBy('word').count()
```

- **Step 4**: Finally the final result will be sent to Stream Output Sink for either storage or for a live dashboard.

```
query = wordCounts.writeStream.outputMode('complete').format('console').
    start()
query.awaitTermination()
```

In this design, Spark Structured Streaming makes sure that the stateful operations like aggregations, joins, windowing, etc. are done consistently and can recover from failure. It uses concepts like Event Time (the time when the data was generated at the source) and Watermarks (a limit on how late a data with certain event time can be accepted) to handle late and out of order data.

The advantages of this programming model are:

- **Ease of use**: The high-level DataFrame and SQL APIs make it simple to implement complex analytics.

- **Event-time processing**: Unlike other systems that process data based on their arrival time, Spark can handle data that arrives late or out of order.

- **Fault-tolerance**: All operations are designed to be fault-tolerance. For stateful operations, it maintains the state across failures.

'Please note that you need to have Spark 2.x in order to utilize structured streaming'.

5.4   How does Spark handle data compression? Discuss the pros and cons of different compression codecs.

Apache Spark supports several types of compression codecs, which can be used to reduce the size of data being stored or transferred, thereby improving speed and saving storage space. Compression in Spark can be applied in various stages including during storage (on HDFS, S3, etc.), during shuffle and cache processes. The choice of the compression codec to use depends on factors such as the nature of the data, the requirements of the specific application, and the specific Spark deployment environment.

Spark supports and can work with the following codecs:

1. **Snappy**: Snappy is an open-source library for compressing and decompressing data. It aims for very high speeds and reasonable compression rather than maximum compression. It's often used for workloads that require fast analytics, such as in-memory computation.

Pros: High compression and decompression speed, reasonable compression ratio.

Cons: Not as efficient in terms of compression factor as some others, such as Gzip.

2. **LZ4**: LZ4 is known for its extremely high speed and efficiency. Like Snappy, it aims for speed and reasonable compression.

Pros: Very high compression and decompression speed.

Cons: It provides less compression ratio than Snappy and Gzip.

3. **Gzip**: Gzip typically achieves better compression than Snappy or LZ4, but is slower.

Pros: High compression ratio, meaning that it often produces smaller files.

Cons: Lower speed of compression and decompression.

4. **LZF**: LZF is a very fast compressor and decompressor when compared to similar competition.

Pros: Offers a good balance between speed and compression ratio.

Cons: Compression and decompression speed is slower than Snappy and LZ4.

5. **Bzip2**: Bzip2 offers the best compression ratio but the worst speed.

Pros: It gives the highest compression ratio among all codecs.

Cons: The cost is its speed - it is the slowest among all listed codecs.

6. **Deflate**: Deflate is a lossless data compression algorithm that uses a combination of the LZ77 algorithm and Huffman coding.

Pros: Has a higher compression ratio than Snappy and LZ4.

Cons: Slower compression and decompression speed when compared to Snappy and LZ4.

7. **Zstandard (or Zstd)**: Zstandard is a real-time compression algorithm, providing high compression ratios with higher speeds. It offers a very wide range of compression/speed trade-off.

Pros: Provides high compression ratio and fast compression and decompression speed.

Cons: A relatively new, it may not support all platforms and libraries.

For setting compression in Spark, one can use the following:

```
# For the spark shell
./bin/spark-shell --conf spark.io.compression.codec=org.apache.spark.io.
    SnappyCompressionCodec
# Within a Spark program
val conf = new SparkConf()
conf.set("spark.io.compression.codec", "org.apache.spark.io.
    SnappyCompressionCodec")
```

While using compression codecs, it's always recommended to test your workload with different codecs and see which one works best for your specific use case: this trade-off between speed and compression factor will depend heavily on the context.

CHAPTER 5. EXPERT   113

5.5 Explain the challenges and solutions for running Spark on a multi-tenant cluster.

Apache Spark is a fast, in-memory data processing engine with development APIs to allow data workers to efficiently execute streaming, machine learning or SQL workloads. However, running Spark on a multi-tenant cluster does present a number of challenges:

1. **Resource Contention**: Resource contention is one of the common challenges in multi-tenant clusters. In a shared environment, different workloads vie for CPU, memory, disk, and bandwidth resources, leading to potential conflict and underperformance.

2. **Managing Workload Diversity**: Each Spark job has its unique resource requirements. Some may be CPU-intensive, others might be I/O-bound or memory-bound. Balancing these diverse workloads on a shared system is a significant operational challenge.

3. **Performance Isolation**: It's important to prevent a resource-intensive process from affecting the performance of other workloads in a multi-tenant environment.

4. **Security and Privacy**: Ensuring that data from one tenant is not accessible to other tenants in the cluster can be challenging.

Here are some possible solutions to these challenges:

1. **Resource Contention**: For resource contention, YARN (Yet Another Resource Negotiator) can be used as a cluster management technology. It allows Spark jobs to run alongside other applications, with resource allocation managed by YARN.

```
spark = SparkSession.builder
    .master("yarn")
    .appName("spark_yarn")
    .getOrCreate()
```

2. **Managing Workload Diversity**: You can use dynamic resource allocation feature in Spark to control the number of executors dynamically based on the workload. You can turn on the dynamic allocation by setting 'spark.dynamicAllocation.enabled' to 'true'.

```
spark.conf.set("spark.dynamicAllocation.enabled", "true")
spark.conf.set("spark.shuffle.service.enabled", "true")
```

3. **Performance Isolation**: Performance isolation can be achieved by leveraging YARN's support for container technology, which encapsulates each Spark job in its own environment. Additionally, Spark's own scheduler can be configured to provide fair sharing of resources across multiple jobs.

4. **Security and Privacy**: Spark's integration with Hadoop includes support for Hadoop's authentication features. The UserGroupInformation class can be used to impersonate a specific user, maintaining data isolation between different jobs on the cluster. Additionally, Spark can also leverage Hadoop's own data access controls (HDFS ACLs/Ranger) to enforce data privacy.

```
from pyspark.sql import SparkSession
from pyspark.sql.types import *
from pyspark.sql.functions import *

UserGroupInformation.loginUserFromKeytab('user@REALM', 'user.keytab')

spark = SparkSession
    .builder
    .appName("multi-tenant example")
    .getOrCreate()

# data access
df = spark.read.text("hdfs://namenode/user/hive/warehouse/test.db/
    test_table")
df.show()
```

Remember, the success of running multiple environments with Spark depends on careful resource management and strict security controls.

5.6 How does Spark's external shuffle service work, and why might you use it?

Apache Spark's shuffle operation redistributes the data across partitions, ensuring that the output is correctly grouped. It's an expensive operation because it could entail a full data transfer over the network.

In the shuffle operation, there are two stages: the map stage and the reduce stage. In the map stage, it writes data into intermediate files. In the reduce stage it fetches that data.

By default, each executor in Spark has a built-in shuffle service. When a shuffle happens, the shuffle service writes shuffle file blocks that are later read by the tasks carrying out the shuffle. The data remains on the executor's local disk until all jobs and stages which need the shuffle data have completed, after which the shuffle files are cleaned up.

The external shuffle service is a separate service which runs one instance per node, independently of the executor. The idea is to have a long-running shuffle service process, external to the executor, monitoring the shuffle files. This has important benefits:

1. Executors can be safely killed, as the shuffle files are not lost with their death. The shuffle service remembers the application ID associated with each shuffle file and can serve requests from executors belonging to the same application. This is particularly essential for Spark's dynamic resource allocation feature where idle executors can be killed and brought back to life later.

2. It reduces network traffic by serving local requests.

Enable the external shuffle service by setting the following configurations:

```
spark.shuffle.service.enabled = true
spark.dynamicAllocation.enabled = true
```

When enabled, each executor will register with the shuffle service on its node and will serve fetch requests from that service. Upon executor death or exit, the shuffle service will continue to serve the shuffle files the executor created.

In conclusion, the external shuffle service ensures that your Spark jobs do not fail because an executor with shuffle files was killed. Its use is crucial when dynamic allocation is utilized but it can also increase the efficiency of shuffling overall when multi-tenancy is implemented.

5.7 Discuss the considerations and best practices for running Spark on cloud platforms like AWS, Azure, or GCP.

Apache Spark can be efficiently run on cloud platforms such as AWS, Azure, or Google Cloud Platform (GCP). Here are some considerations and best practices:

1. **Use Cloud-Optimized Data Formats and Storage**: Apache Spark has inbuilt support for a multitude of data formats. Binary file formats such as Parquet, Avro, and ORC are recommended. They're highly optimized for use in cloud environments. Consider using cloud-based storage like S3 for AWS, Blob Storage for Azure or Cloud Storage for GCP.

2. **Managing Compute Resources**: Provision your Spark clusters to match your workload requirements. Cloud platforms offer several instance types with different CPU, memory, storage, and networking capabilities. Control the size of the cluster (number of nodes) and pick appropriate VM types on the basis of the workload.

3. **Use Elasticity of Cloud**: Take advantage of the cloud's elasticity. Spark clusters can be dynamically resized on many cloud platforms. Scale up during periods of high demand and scale down during periods of low demand or inactivity to save costs.

4. **Data Locality**: To reduce costs and improve performance, it's generally recommended to run your computations as close to your data as possible. Check whether your cloud provider charges for data transfer between regions or different services.

5. **Use Managed Spark Services**: These services like EMR (for AWS), HDInsight (for Azure), or Dataproc (for GCP) greatly simplify the setup, management, and scaling of Spark clusters.

6. **Security**: Ensure sensitive data is encrypted, both at rest and in transit. Also, control access to Spark jobs and data using IAM roles and permissions.

7. **Monitoring and Troubleshooting**: Use cloud-specific monitoring tools like CloudWatch (AWS), Stackdriver (GCP), and Azure Monitor for full visibility into your Spark applications.

8. **Tune Spark for the Cloud**: Tune Spark parameters to optimize for network latency, disk I/O, and data serialization/deserialization.

For example, in AWS EMR:

```
spark = (
    SparkSession.builder
    .appName("spark_on_aws")
    .config("spark.executor.instances", "5")
    .config("spark.executor.memory", "4g")
    .config("spark.driver.memory", "2g")
    .config("spark.executor.cores", "3")
    .getOrCreate()
)
```

In this example, we are creating a SparkSession with an application name "spark_on_aws", setting the number of executor instances to 5, and allocating memory and cores for executors and driver.

Remember, running Spark on the cloud typically involves trade-offs between cost and performance. It's essential to monitor and adjust your settings to find what works best for your specific workload.

Coming back to managed Spark services like EMR, HDInsight or Dataproc. They're integrated in RBAC systems of AWS, Azure and

Google Cloud respectively. EMR supports IAM roles, HDInsight can be integrated with Azure Active Directory and Dataproc utilises Google Cloud IAM.

For monitoring: - In EMR, you can monitor your Spark applications using Amazon CloudWatch. - Azure provides HDInsight Cluster monitoring through Azure Monitor and Log Analytics. - Google Cloud's Dataproc jobs and clusters can be monitored with Stackdriver.

If your data is large, consider using the larger instance sizes that provide more memory and CPU resources to handle the data processing.

Keep in mind that pricing models differ from vendor to vendor. Always check the pricing models of each cloud provider before migrating your Spark applications to the cloud.

5.8   How do you handle data security and encryption in Spark, both in transit and at rest?

Apache Spark provides several mechanisms to secure data both during transit and at rest. Here are some common ways of handling data security and encryption in Spark:

1. **Data Encryption**:

Spark natively doesn't perform data encryption either during transit or at rest. Therefore, to achieve data encryption, we use Hadoop Distributed File System (HDFS) or some other secure storage system which supports encryption. HDFS supports native encryption for data at rest. Moreover, for data in transit, HDFS supports Secure Socket Layer/Transport Layer Security (SSL/TLS).

Configuration for encryption at rest and in transit can be done in

HDFS like shown below:

```
<property>
  <name>dfs.encrypt.data.transfer</name>
  <value>true</value>
</property>
```

2. **Authentication**:

Apache Spark supports Kerberos authentication. It uses Simple Authentication and Security Layer (SASL) and a pluggable mechanism for authentication, authorization, encryption and token generation. For instance:

```
<property>
  <name>spark.authenticate</name>
  <value>true</value>
</property>
```

Authentication can also be set up for the Spark Thrift server using the below configuration:

```
<property>
  <name>hive.server2.authentication</name>
  <value>KERBEROS</value>
</property>
```

3. **Authorization**:

Apache Spark supports access control on resources. Users can set permissions for directories and files in HDFS which is the primary file storage for spark. In HDFS, permission for directories and files can be set by the following command.

```
hadoop fs -chmod 700 /path/to/directory
```

And for Spark SQL, access control can be configured at table and column level by using Apache Ranger or Apache Sentry.

4. **Auditing**:

Apache Spark does not natively support auditing but it can use auditing capabilities of underlying storage system like HDFS. Again, open source tools like Apache Ranger could be used for auditing purposes.

In conclusion, although Apache Spark offers several security features like authentication and authorization, the current implementation for data encryption is heavily dependent on the underlying storage system (like HDFS) or other tools like Apache Ranger or Apache Sentry.

5.9   Explain the role of the Block Manager in Spark's architecture.

Block Manager is a crucial component of Spark's architecture, responsible for managing the data storage and retrieval aspects on the Spark worker nodes. It essentially operates as a cache layer between your Spark tasks and the storage system (which can be HDFS, local disk, or others).

Every Spark executor (JVM process running on a worker node) has a Block Manager which controls approximately all memory storage. Some of the key roles played by Spark Block Manager are outlined as follows:

1. **Storage and Retrieval:** Block Manager provides interfaces to put, retrieve and remove blocks, and it also transfers blocks (data) from the local node to any other node. This action is significant during the Shuffle phase in Spark's computations.

2. **Disk Persistence:** Block Manager has the capability to use off-heap memory or disk space for storing RDD blocks. This means that data which doesn't fit into memory can be moved to disk.

3. **In-Memory Storage:** Block Manager keeps RDD partitions in serialized and unserialized formats in memory. This feature enhances the processing speed of Spark applications as they don't have to read data from disk storage latency.

4. **Data Locality:** Block Manager plays a key role in achieving

data locality. It's aware of the locations of all data blocks and helps schedule tasks closer to the data they operate on.

5. **Cache Management:** Block Manager manages the cache, making decisions on what data to cache and what data to evict when memory is limited.

Below is an instance of how you interact with Block Manager when you persist an RDD:

```
# Assume an RDD
rdd = sc.parallelize(range(10))

# Caching the RDD
rdd.persist()
```

When calling the persist method on an RDD, you notify the Block Manager to cache the RDD partitions. For every cached partition, a block is created, storing the partition data. The Block Manager enables the retrieval of the stored blocks when actions are performed on the cached RDD, which means no need to recompute the data.

Remember, though, that Block Manager is low-level module and most users interact with RDD/Dataset/DataFrame APIs, not directly with the Block Manager. The Spark does the plumbing and orchestration.

5.10 How can you optimize Spark applications for large-scale shuffles?

Optimizing Spark applications for large-scale shuffles can be a crucial step in improving efficiency, as shuffling is a computationally expensive operation. Here are a few steps that can be taken:

1. **Avoid operations that trigger shuffles**: Shuffles are triggered by operations like 'groupByKey','reduceByKey','join', etc. Alternate methods should be considered that do not trigger shuffles. For example, using 'reduceByKey' instead of 'groupByKey' can combine output with a common key on each partition before shuffling the

data.

2. **Tune the Spark Shuffle partitions**: The number of partitions
to use when shuffling data for joins or aggregations can be modified.
Spark defaults to 200 partitions, but this setting can be tuned based
on the size of your cluster and the amount of data. You can set this
property using 'spark.sql.shuffle.partitions' to an appropriate number
for your data.

```
spark.conf.set("spark.sql.shuffle.partitions", "500")
```

3. **Use 'broadcast' variable**: If one of the data frames involved
in the shuffle operation is small enough to fit into the memory of a
single worker node in its entirety, we can mark the data frame as a
'broadcast variable'. It will make Spark replicate the data frame on
all worker nodes and will eliminate the need for shuffling the data
across machines.

```
from pyspark.sql.functions import broadcast
largeDF.join(broadcast(smallDF), "key")
```

4. **Persist RDDs/DataFrames/Datasets**: If an RDD/DataFrame/-
Dataset is reused in computations, it is useful to persist it in memory
using the 'persist()' or 'cache()' method.

```
df.persist()
```

5. **Increasing Parallelism**: Shuffling is an expensive operation due
to the repartition of data across the network. But we can increase
the number of partitions to reduce network congestion. This can be
achieved with 'spark.default.parallelism' and 'spark.sql.shuffle.partitions'.

```
spark.conf.set("spark.default.parallelism", "100")
```

6. **Salting Technique**: In case of skewed data, salting is a technique where we add an additional key to the data. This additional
key helps in randomly distributing data to avoid skewed partitions.

Remember, these are general tips and they need to be tested and validated with your specific use case as each Spark application can behave differently based on the nature of the data and the operations being performed.

5.11 Discuss the intricacies of Spark's cost-based optimizer and its impact on query performance.

Apache Spark is renowned for its Catalyst Optimizer, which is essentially a Cost-Based Optimizer (CBO). Like other database systems, Spark employs this optimizer to decide the most efficient way to execute a Spark SQL query. To lessen the time and computation of executing a Spark SQL operation, the optimizer builds a logical plan and generates several physical execution plans.

These plans are evaluated using a cost model to select the most effective execution plan. Cost here refers to the resources like CPU, I/O, network I/O, etc., required for executing the plan.

This optimizer employs data statistics to select the most effective plan. It covers operations like selection, projection, and join. However, it's important to note that these statistics need to be computed and stored in the metadata of the table which is achieved by the command 'ANALYZE TABLE COMPUTE STATISTICS'.

For instance, when joining multiple tables, the Catalyst Optimizer considers the size of the tables, their column statistics (e.g., min, max, numNulls, distinctCount, avgLen, maxLen), and even the relationship between the columns. Using all these details, the Optimizer decides the order of joining the tables and the type of join (Broadcast, Sort Merge, Hash, etc.). Let's take a code snippet for clarity:

```
spark.sql("ANALYZE TABLE sales COMPUTE STATISTICS")
spark.sql("ANALYZE TABLE sales COMPUTE STATISTICS FOR COLUMNS sales_person_id
    , product_id")
```

Here, 'ANALYZE TABLE COMPUTE STATISTICS' computes statistics for tables, and 'ANALYZE TABLE COMPUTE STATISTICS FOR COLUMNS' compute column-level statistics for Spark to make better planning decisions. Going forward, all Spark SQL queries against the 'sales' table will leverage these statistics when available.

Adding to this is the concept of Spark's Adaptive Query Execution (AQE), which further enhances the query performance by dynamically modifying the execution plan at runtime based on the actual performance statistics of the executed stages.

With the evolution of Spark and enhancements in its Optimizer, it has become more and more effective in optimizing the queries, thereby significantly improving the performance of Spark applications. However, understanding the intricacies of how the Optimizer works will be increasingly beneficial for developers and analysts to write better and optimized Spark code.

5.12   How do you handle backpressure in Spark Streaming?

Backpressure is a mechanism that is used in Spark Streaming to control the rate of incoming data to ensure that the rate of inputs does not overwhelm the processing capacity of the system, thereby preventing the system from running out of memory.

Spark's backpressure feature, as of version 1.5, helps to dynamically adjust the data ingestion rates in Spark Streaming. If backpressure is enabled, the system automatically calculates and sets the ingestion rate, thereby preventing the system from being overwhelmed with data. In a layman terms, backpressure keeps the data queue from getting too large.

You can enable backpressure by setting the 'spark.streaming. backpressure.enabled' configuration property to 'true'. Here is a sample code snippet:

```
from pyspark import SparkConf, SparkContext
from pyspark.streaming import StreamingContext

# Set up the Spark configuration with the backpressure feature enabled
conf = SparkConf().setAppName("SparkStreamWithBackpressure").setMaster("local
    [*]").set("spark.streaming.backpressure.enabled", "true")
sc = SparkContext(conf=conf)
ssc = StreamingContext(sc, 1)
```

You can also set the initial rate of data ingestion when backpressure is enabled using the 'spark.streaming.backpressure.initialRate' property.

```
conf.set("spark.streaming.backpressure.initialRate", "5000")
```

An alternative method to handle backpressure without enabling Spark's backpressure feature is to control the data input rate at the source e.g., Kafka, Flume etc.

But, remember to tune the system appropriately because improper configuration could still result in the system running out of memory or other resource contention issues. Other related parameters that can be adjusted are 'spark.streaming.receiver.maxRate', 'spark.streaming. kafka.maxRatePerPartition' etc., which restrict the maximum rates at which data is received.

5.13   Describe the process of tuning garbage collection for a Spark application.

The garbage collection (GC) for a Spark application refers to the process of managing memory in the JVM heap by detecting and deleting objects that are no longer in use. The goal of GC tuning is to minimize the time that the application spends on GC activity.

Here are some steps to tune Garbage Collection for a Spark Application:

1. **Monitor your application for GC issues:** It's important to

monitor your application to identify if it is spending an excessive time performing GC. You can use Spark web UI, or the GC logs of the JVM. If the GC time is high, then it is an indication that GC tuning may be necessary.

2. **Choose appropriate GC algorithm:** You need to select a garbage collector that is suitable for your needs. There are different types of garbage collectors available, such as ParallelGC, ConcMarkSweepGC and G1GC. By default, Spark uses the ParallelGC. If your Spark application has a large heap size and you want to limit GC pauses, you might choose the G1GC.

```
spark-submit --conf "spark.executor.extraJavaOptions=-XX:+UseG1GC" ...
```

3. **Tune heap size:** Proper tuning of the heap size can help to improve GC performance. The heap space is divided into Young and Old generations. The Young Generation is where all new objects are created. When the young generation is filled, a minor GC is performed. If Spark jobs run out of JVM heap memory, consider increasing spark.driver.memory for the driver process and spark.executor.memory for the executor process.

```
spark-submit --conf "spark.driver.memory=4g" --conf "spark.executor.memory
    =16g" ...
```

4. **Tune spark.memory.fraction:** Spark allows you to specify the fraction of heap space to use for execution and storage inside a JVM process. The spark.memory.fraction parameter determines the proportion of heap space to use for Spark's memory cache. A lower value means more heap space is available for Spark to use but less for user data structures, functions, and variables directly tied to Spark tasks. You need to find a balance according to your application's specific needs.

```
spark-submit --conf "spark.memory.fraction=0.6" ...
```

5. **Minimize object allocations:** If an application creates a lot of temporary objects, it can lead to frequent GCs. To reduce the frequency of GC, you should minimize the creation of temporary objects

in your Spark Application.

Remember, GC tuning involves trade-offs and requires a deep understanding of how your application works and the characteristics of your data. It's best to thoroughly test any changes in a controlled environment before rolling them out to your production system.

5.14 How does Spark integrate with GPU resources for accelerated computation?

Since Spark 3.0, Apache Spark offers the capability to accelerate computation by utilizing Graphics Processing Units (GPUs). This feature is mainly aimed at aiding tasks that involve machine learning and data science oriented workloads, as these tasks often carry heavy computations that can be efficiently handled by GPUs.

The GPU scheduling and isolation capabilities are currently available for standalone mode and Kubernetes (starting from Apache Spark 3.1.1). It is not yet fully integrated for other resource managers like YARN or Mesos.

Here is the basic architecture of how Spark integrates with GPU:

- Application Level Scheduling: Within a Spark application, when a task is scheduled to run on a GPU-enabled executor, the task will run on one of the available GPUs on that executor.

- Executor Level Scheduling: When Spark launches executors, it can request GPU resources from cluster managers (either Standalone or Kubernetes) to launch the executor. If the cluster manager supports GPU scheduling, it will allocate specific GPUs to the Spark executor.

You can specify the amount of GPU resources per executor and per task while submitting the Spark application. Here's a code example:

```
./bin/spark-submit --executor-cores=1 --conf "spark.executor.resource.gpu.
    amount=1" --conf "spark.task.resource.gpu.amount=0.33" ...
```

In this example, you're specifying that each executor gets 1 GPU and each task gets 0.33 of a GPU (i.e., you can run three tasks concurrently per GPU).

Below is a configuration example when Spark runs on Kubernetes:

```
spark.kubernetes.executor.request.gpu=1
spark.executor.resource.gpu.amount=1
```

This shows that Spark will request 1 GPU for each executor from the Kubernetes cluster.

Please note that, in order to use this feature, the GPU versions of the necessary libraries like CUDA need to be installed across the cluster. Spark does not handle the installation of these dependencies and expects these to be properly set up.

5.15   Discuss the challenges and strategies for ETL operations in Spark, especially with large and diverse datasets.

Extract, Transform and Load (ETL) operations are crucial in data warehousing. In Apache Spark, ETL operations can sometimes be challenging, especially when dealing with large and diverse datasets.

Challenges:

1. **Resource Management:** Unlike relational database management systems, Apache Spark keeps most of the dataset in-memory, which provides faster access and processing time. However, when working with large datasets, memory management can become a challenge.

2. **Schema Inference:** When the structure of the data is not known in advance, Spark has to infer the schema of the dataset. This operation can be computationally expensive in terms of time and resources

for large datasets.

3. **Data Skewness:** Data skewness can affect the performance of Spark operations. If some of the data values are more frequent than others, data skewness can slow down the job and can cause out of memory errors.

4. **Data Quality Issues:** Diverse datasets bring diverse data quality issues. Handling missing data, incorrect data types, and format issues can pose a significant challenge.

Strategies:

1. **Partitioning:** To mitigate the challenges of resource management and data skewness, data partitioning effectively divides data into smaller, manageable portions.

```
df = spark.read.csv("large_dataset.csv")
df.repartition(10)
```

2. **Persist and Checkpoint:** Persist operation allows intermediate data to be stored in memory or disk for faster access. Meanwhile, checkpointing saves the RDD to disk and truncates the lineage graph. This is particularly useful for iterative algorithms that create long lineage graphs.

```
intermediate_rdd.persist()
intermediate_rdd.checkpoint()
```

3. **Broadcast Variables:** If there are smaller datasets that are being used in multiple stages, one can 'broadcast' them, i.e., cache them on each worker. This can drastically improve the speed of joins or any operation that requires shuffling.

```
broadcastVar = spark.sparkContext.broadcast([1, 2, 3])
```

4. **Schema Specification:** Instead of inferring schema, specifying schema programmatically will speed up the ETL process.

```
from pyspark.sql.types import *
```

```
schema = StructType([
    StructField("name", StringType()),
    StructField("age", IntegerType()),
    StructField("city", StringType())
])

df = spark.read.csv("large_dataset.csv", schema=schema)
```

5. **Handling Data Quality:** Spark provides powerful APIs for dealing with data quality issues. Functions such as 'na.fill()', 'na.drop()', and 'cast()' comes in handy when dealing with missing values, data types problems, etc.

```
df = df.na.fill(value='UNKNOWN', subset=['city'])
df = df.na.drop()
df = df.withColumn("age", df["age"].cast(IntegerType()))
```

6. **Avoiding Operations That Trigger Shuffling:** Certain operations like 'distinct()', 'groupBy()', 'join()' cause data shuffling which is an expensive operation. Try to minimize these operations or if possible, perform them on a smaller portion of the data.

By using these strategies, the above-mentioned challenges can be mitigated, thus making ETL operations in Spark efficient and robust.

5.16 How do you handle stateful operations in Spark Streaming, especially over long windows of time?

Stateful operations in Spark Streaming are those operations that track data across time. They're crucial for many real-time applications. An example would be: Keep a track of the "last seen" time of a user activity in a stream of data. These are not easy to implement at scale as efficiently saving, retrieving and updating such state information can be difficult, especially if the state is too large to fit in memory.

Spark Streaming provides a powerful programming model, called window operations, for processing data over sliding windows, which is stateful. However, in addition, Spark Streaming provides two high-level operations for data that goes beyond simple windows - 'updateStateByKey' and 'mapWithState'.

The 'updateStateByKey' operation allows us to maintain arbitrary state while continuously updating it with new information. It requires defining a state, an initial RDD for the state and a state update function.

```
def updateFunc(new_values, last_sum):
    return sum(new_values) + (last_sum or 0)

runningCounts = stream.updateStateByKey(updateFunc)
```

'mapWithState' is a more efficient version which provides more control on the timeout of the state. The mapWithState operation is used to track these time-based aggregations.

```
def updateFunc(batchTime, key, value, state):
    # does something with state and value
    return (key, some_value)

stateSpec = StateSpec.function(updateFunc).numPartitions(10)
mappedstream = stream.mapWithState(stateSpec)
```

Note that, these stateful operations, require enabling a checkpoint directory where it will stores the state information, as the state can recover to a previous point in case of failure.

The disadvantage of these operations is they don't scale well to large application state. For long windows of time, or when the application state is large, you may encounter memory issues if you are not careful, because state can grow indefinitely. These cases can be handled by batch interval and window duration. You can specify the timeouts state. In a typical use case, the state may depend only on a particular window of past data, and after that window, the state may not be useful anymore. With these cases, you can set a sliding interval for calculating the transformations.

One solution for dealing with large state or long windows can be using the 'Timeout' parameter with 'mapWithState' which allows us to define when we want the state to age out, e.g 'StateSpec.function(

mappingFunction).timeout(Milliseconds(12000)))'.

To manage the state over a long window of time, you might also need to adjust other parameters, like the batch size, to ensure Spark has enough resources to correctly perform these operations.

5.17 Explain the impact of data locality on Spark's performance and strategies to optimize it.

Data locality is a critical aspect in Apache Spark that greatly affects the performance. It refers to the ability to move the computation close to where the actual data resides on the node, instead of moving large amounts of data over the network, which can be costly.

There are different levels of data locality, including:

1. PROCESS_LOCAL: Data and computation reside on the same JVM.

2. NODE_LOCAL: Data and computation reside on the same node.

3. NO_PREF: No preference for data's location.

4. RACK_LOCAL: Data and computation reside on the same rack.

5. ANY: Data can be anywhere, even on a different datacenter.

Spark takes this into account during scheduling tasks in Spark applications. Tasks are scheduled on the node where the data resides. The scheduler will wait for a short time to try scheduling on the same node or the same rack before it gives up and uses a farther data location.

A Spark job's performance can heavily depend on network bandwidth and data locality. If there is no data locality, the increased use of resources (network I/O and CPU mainly) may easily lead to a bottleneck, increasing the delay in task completion.

Optimization Strategies for Data Locality in Spark:

1. Increasing Spark locality wait time: Increasing the spark.locality.wait parameter's value can enhance data locality, thus improving the performance.

```
spark = SparkSession.builder
    .config("spark.locality.wait", "10s")
    .getOrCreate()
```

2. Minimize the data shuffling: Avoiding operations like groupByKey, reduceByKey etc. that trigger shuffling of data. This should be avoided because it can force Spark to fetch data from remote nodes if it doesn't exist locally. Instead of reduceByKey, use functions like combineByKey which perform combining locally on each mapper before sending the results to reducers.

3. Using broadcast variables: Another way is to use Broadcast variables to send a read-only variable to the workers, which can be cached on those nodes and not sent over the network multiple times.

```
broadcastVar = spark.sparkContext.broadcast([1, 2, 3])
```

4. Repartitioning: Repartitioning the data. Partitioning can control data locality. By repartitioning the data, you can ensure that related data is stored together at the same node.

```
df.repartition(10)
```

With careful attention to data locality, Spark applications can be made much more efficient, simply by reducing data movement over the network.

5.18 How do you ensure exactly-once semantics in Spark Streaming applications?

Exactly once semantics is a desirable property in distributed streaming system where each record is processed exactly once, meaning no data will be missed and no data will be processed more than once.

In Spark Streaming, to ensure exactly-once semantics you need to
ensure two things: 1) Data receiving: Data should be received exactly
once by the receiver of Spark Streaming application from sources like
Kafka, Flume, and Kinesis etc. This can be achieved by using Write
Ahead Logs (WAL) in Spark Streaming. WAL synchronizes the data
received from the receiver to a log file before processing it. This
ensures that all the data has been logged in a fault-tolerant manner
apart from in-memory storage. So, if a worker node dies, the logged
data can be used for recovery.

2) Data processing: Data processed by the Spark Streaming application should reflect in the final output exactly once. This means
the transformation and output operations should be idempotent to
handle reprocessing. Spark provides 'updateStateByKey' operation
which gives access to the state variable representing the history of an
RDD. It ensures fault-tolerance and maintains consistency in output.

Here is an example of how to use it:

```
def updateFunc(new_values, last_sum):
    return sum(new_values) + (last_sum or 0)

running_counts = pairs.updateStateByKey(updateFunc)
```

Another approach to achieve exactly-once semantics is to store the
state and metadata information in a reliable and transactional data
store system such as a database or a filesystem. This way, if a batch
of data needs to be reprocessed, both the processing state and the
already processed data can be rolled back, ensuring exactly-once semantics.

It should be noted that while Spark Streaming provides the tools to
ensure exactly-once semantics, it requires careful design of the Spark
Streaming application.

5.19 Discuss the role and configuration of the spark.cleaner. referenceTracking.cleanCheckpoints parameter.

The 'spark.cleaner.referenceTracking.cleanCheckpoints' parameter is a configuration setting available in Apache Spark. It controls whether automatic periodic cleaning for checkpoints data is enabled or not. This parameter, by default, is set to 'false'.

Checkpoints in Apache Spark provide fault-tolerance for long running computations. During the computations, in intermediate stages, data is checkpointed i.e., saved to reliable storage (like the Hadoop Distributed File System (HDFS)) to avoid the re-computation of lost data. However, the checkpointed data can consume a substantial amount of storage.

If the storage consumption becomes a concern, you may want to clean up old checkpoint data.
This is where the 'spark.cleaner.referenceTracking.cleanCheckpoints' parameter comes in. By setting this parameter to 'true', Spark will automatically clean up the old checkpoint data.

Here's how you should configure it in your Spark application:

```
val sparkConf = new SparkConf().setAppName("Spark App")
sparkConf.set("spark.cleaner.referenceTracking.cleanCheckpoints", "true")
val sc = new SparkContext(sparkConf)
```

The above code turns on the automatic checkpoint cleaning. Bear in mind that once you have enabled this Spark feature, it will delete all the checkpoint data that's no longer being referred to by the application.

As for the role, remember that a Spark application's configuration can greatly influence the performance. Having unnecessary data stored in your storage could slow down some operations or even make the storage get full. Therefore, properly tuning configuration parameters, including 'spark.cleaner.referenceTracking.cleanCheckpoints', according to the specific needs of your Spark application can help improve its performance and resource usage.

5.20   How do you handle version compatibility issues, especially when integrating Spark with evolving external systems or libraries?

Version compatibility issues while integrating Spark with evolving external systems or libraries can be challenging. Here are some strategies to handle them:

1. **Check Official Documentation**: One of the initial steps is to always refer to the official documentation of both Apache Spark and that of the external system or library. This contains a lot of critical information about the versions they are compatible with.

2. **Using the Right Spark Packages**: Spark has a package system (Spark Packages), which is a community-based repository for Spark Libraries and Tools. It's recommended to use the packages from here and carefully checking the versions they support; ensuring they work well with the version of Spark you're using.

3. **Building Spark with Correct Profile**: When building Spark from source, it is essential to use the right build profile to match the version of Hadoop you are using. Spark can be built to work with a specific version of Hadoop using build properties. For example, you can build Spark for Hadoop 2.7 using 'sbt -Pyarn -Phadoop-2.7'

```
./build/mvn -Pyarn -Phadoop-2.7 -DskipTests clean package
```

4. **Testing**: It is highly recommended to thoroughly test your Spark application after any version change. This can help to identify

both runtime and compile-time conflicts.

5. **Using Compatibility Layers**: You can use compatibility layers or bridges to interact between various versions of your systems. For instance, when using Apache Kafka with Spark, you might consider using a tool like Schema Registry which provides a RESTful interface for managing and applying versioned Avro schemas to data in Kafka.

6. **Use Docker Containers**: Another way to handle versioning issues is to use Docker containers, where each container would handle a certain version of Spark along with its dependencies.

7. **Dependency Management Tools**: Consider using software tools such as Maven or SBT for managing project dependencies. They can help in identifying and resolving conflicting dependencies.

Remember, the version compatibility is an ongoing issue in the evolving Big Data ecosystem with every minor or major version potentially introducing a breaking change. It's always highly recommended to stay updated with the version details from either the product release notes or official documentation.

Chapter 6

Guru

6.1 Describe in detail the internal workings of the Catalyst optimizer, including rule-based and cost-based optimizations.

The Catalyst Optimizer is an integral part of Apache Spark which applies a series of rule-based and cost-based optimization techniques to generate an efficient execution plan for a given logical plan or SQL query.

At first glance, the Catalyst Optimizer can be seen as a compiler that translates a high-level SQL query into a low-level RDD operation. However, it does much more than this. The entire process can be segmented into four major steps:

1. Analysis
2. Logical Optimization

3. Physical Planning

4. Code Generation.

1. Analysis:

In this stage, Catalyst converts raw SQL strings into an Abstract Syntax Tree (AST), resolves identifiers (i.e., tables and columns) against the catalog, and performs type checking. Catalyst supports for both SQL and DataFrame API semantics in the same engine.

```
from pyspark.sql import SparkSession

spark = SparkSession.builder
    .appName('Catalyst Optimizer')
    .getOrCreate()

df = spark.read.csv("data.csv", header=True, inferSchema=True)

df.createOrReplaceTempView("data")

spark.sql("SELECT * FROM data").explain(True)
```

2. Logical Optimization:

Catalyst applies a series of rule-based optimizations on the logical plan to achieve better performance. These optimization techniques involve constant folding, predicate pushdown, projection pruning, NULL propagation, boolean simplification and others.

Catalyst uses a feature called 'tree transformation framework' in a modular way where developers can insert new optimization techniques and improve the existing ones.

3. Physical Planning:

In this stage, Catalyst will generate multiple physical plans from the logical plan. Here comes the cost-based optimizer which picks the optimal physical plan based on the cost model.

Physical plan operators include sorts, joins, aggregations etc. It will make several versions of plans and chooses the plan with least cost based on the cost model.

#**4.Code Generation:**

Finally, Catalyst will produce bytecode that can run on the Java Virtual Machine (JVM) to execute the selected physical execution plan.

Catalyst uses 'whole-stage code generation' to produce compact JVM bytecode. It eliminates the cost of virtual function dispatches and leverages CPU pipelining and cache memory efficiently.

In a nutshell, the core mission of Catalyst optimizer is to leverage advanced programming language features to build an extensible query optimization framework. It is designed in such a way that adding new optimization techniques and improving the existing ones is much simpler.

6.2 How does Spark's Tungsten engine manage binary processing and memory management at the byte level?

Apache Spark's Tungsten project aims to enhance the efficiency of Spark applications by exploiting modern compilers and CPUs to manage and manipulate data at the binary level.

When it comes to binary processing, Tungsten represents data using binary format for compact storage in memory or serialized over the network. By binary processing, it eliminates the overheads of JVM object model, garbage collection, and also enables more efficient data compression and serialization. This significantly aids in improving the memory usage and computational speed of Spark jobs.

The sample code below demonstrates how Spark employs Tungsten for binary processing :

```
val df = spark.range(1 * 1000 * 1000).toDF("id").withColumn("square", col("id
    ") * col("id"))
```

```
df.cache()
df.count()
```

In terms of memory management, Tungsten bypasses the Java Garbage Collector entirely by implementing a custom memory management layer. Instead of relying on the JVM's object model and its garbage collector, Spark manages memory explicitly within a large, long-lived array of bytes. This is particularly useful in high-performance computing and on modern hardware where memory access patterns can have a profound impact on computation speeds.

The Tungsten's memory management is divided into two pools: execution and storage. Execution refers to the computation of tasks, while storage corresponds to caching and propagating internal data across the cluster. Both pools can borrow memory from each other up to a certain limit.

Here is how it's typically represented:

```
---------------------------------------------------
|       Execution       |       Storage       |
---------------------------------------------------
```

The dynamic allocation enables Spark to utilize memory resources better, reduce out-of-memory errors, and execute tasks more quickly. It also minimizes overhead, which is particularly important in iterative computations common in machine learning and graph computations.

Tungsten uses a technique named "binary in-memory data representation" and "explicit memory management (for both storage and execution)" which aids in achieving the aforementioned efficiencies. Both of these techniques work at the byte level, hence reducing the random memory access patterns significantly, and thus providing faster data processing, particularly for large datasets.

6.3   Dive deep into the intricacies of Spark's shuffle operations. How are they implemented at the byte level, and how do they manage data spill-over?

Apache Spark's shuffle operation is a mechanism that redistributes the data across different partitions. More specifically, it involves the re-distribution of data so that data on the same key ends up on the same partition.

The shuffle operation mainly consists of the following phases:

1. **Map Side:** During the map phase, as soon as the map-side computation is done on a partition, Spark writes the intermediate result to a local disk before it sends the results over the network to the reducer. These intermediate results are a sequence of serialized binary rows. The serialization is done using the Kryo serializer (or Java serializer), converting the objects to a byte array.

```
val rdd = sc.textFile("path")
val map = rdd.flatMap(line => line.split("␣")).map(word => (word,1))
val reduce = map.reduceByKey(_+_)
```

In the above example, reduceByKey operation would cause a shuffle. During the shuffle, Spark would write the map output to local disk in serialized binary rows.

2. **Reduce Side:** This is the side that receives the shuffled data. The reducer does not start until all the maps are done since the reducer needs to pull all of the relevant data. At the reducer side, the serialized data which is read from the disk are de-serialized back to the original data type/objects.

The concept of Shuffle Spill:

Spark has two configurations, 'spark.shuffle.spill' and 'spark.shuffle.memoryFraction' that govern how Spark uses and controls the memory during the shuffle process.

Spilling can be understood as Spark's mechanism to hand-off the data to the disk whenever it thinks it is running out of memory. When Spark decides to spill, it sorts the data and writes it to the disk. Consequently, multiple spills will generate multiple sorted files, which will eventually be merge sorted. Spilling is an expensive operation, it involves CPU and IO time, as well as the time taken for writing the data to the disk.

* 'spark.shuffle.spill' is a flag to specify whether the memory should be spilled during shuffles. By default, its value is set to true.

* 'spark.shuffle.memoryFraction' expresses the size of the shuffle buffer as a fraction of total heap size. This buffer is used when serializing the map output during shuffles, so it can be very important for maintaining high performance if you have a large amount of map output.

In conclusion, Apache Spark's shuffle operation is a crucial part of the computational flow. It enables efficient re-distribution of data across the partitions. However, care should be taken to handle the shuffle operation effectively because it can easily become a bottleneck in the system if not handled efficiently. In particular, managing data spill-over during shuffle operation is critical for maintaining the performance and stability of the system.

6.4 Discuss the challenges and solutions for ensuring data lineage in large-scale Spark applications.

Data lineage in Spark, or any other data-centric application refers to the series of operations that led to a particular data artifact's present state. It is a way of tracking information about the input sources, transformations, and output data. Data lineage plays a key role in root cause analysis, data quality assessment, impact analysis, and legal or regulatory compliance among others. It proves to be critical

in large-scale Spark applications, say, while debugging or in situations
dealing with ETL (Extract, Transform, Load) processes.

Challenges:

1. Complexity: In large-scale Spark applications, tracking the transformations applied to each RDD isn't straightforward due to the complexity
of the data flow.

2. Volume: High volumes of data being processed and transferred between
stages add to the complexity of ensuring data lineage.

3. System Infrastructure: Spark lacks built-in capabilities for maintaining
detailed data lineage information.

4. Efficiency and Performance: Storing extensive details regarding every
operation performed on the dataset can degrade the system efficiency and
performance.

Solutions: To tackle these challenges, you might have to integrate
Spark with third-party data lineage tools or build custom functionality within your Spark applications. Here are a few methodologies
that could be employed:

1. Using Accumulators and Broadcast Variables:

- Accumulators could be used to debug applications. Spark actions and
transformations can be accumulated and analyzed later for error investi-
gation.

- Broadcast variables allow the programmer to keep a read-only variable
cached on each machine rather than shipping a copy of it with tasks.

```
val accum = sc.longAccumulator("My Accumulator")
sc.parallelize(Array(1, 2, 3, 4)).foreach(x => accum.add(x))
println(accum.value) // prints 10
```

2. Apache Atlas:

- is a scalable and extensible set of core foundational governance services that enables organizations to effectively and efficiently meet their
compliance requirements within Hadoop and allows integration with the
complete enterprise data ecosystem.

3. Spline:

- An open-source data lineage tracking and visualization solution for Apache Spark. Spline captures and visualizes data lineage information automatically and provides an interactive lineage diagram where one can explore transformations in detail.

```
val sparkSession: SparkSession = SparkSession.builder()
  .appName("Example")
  .getOrCreate()

import za.co.absa.spline.harvester.SparkLineageInitializer._
sparkSession.enableLineageTracking()

val df = sparkSession.read
  .format("csv")
  .option("header", "true")
  .load("data.csv")

df.filter($"_c0" > 10)
  .write
  .format("parquet")
  .mode("overwrite")
  .save("output.parquet")
```

4. Custom Logging and Monitoring: This could include logging transformations and actions or tracking the RDD transformations using Spark listener interfaces or accumulators.

In summary, ensuring data lineage in large-scale Spark applications is a challenging task but it's an essential part of data governance. There's no one-size-fits-all solution to this challenge and the approach should be chosen carefully considering the specific requirements and constraints of the project.

6.5 How does Spark's Structured Streaming handle late data and stateful processing at scale?

Apache Spark's Structured Streaming provides two key mechanisms for dealing with late data and stateful processing at scale: watermarking and mapGroupsWithState or flatMapGroupsWithState operations.

Watermarking is a method to specify the threshold of late data. It allows the Spark engine to assume that the data should have arrived by a certain time and it is used to limit the amount of old data that needs to be considered for handling late data. It helps to handle incomplete data or data that comes out of order (either because it was produced out of order or because it was delivered out of order).

Here is an example of how you might use watermarking:

```
// Read data from Kafka
val streaming = spark
.readStream
.format("kafka")
.option("kafka.bootstrap.servers", "host1:port1,host2:port2")
.option("subscribe", "updates")
.load()

// Parse data and add timestamp
val data = streaming
.selectExpr("CAST(value AS STRING)")
.select(from_json($"value", schema) as "updates")
.select("updates.*")
.select($"eventId", $"eventTime".cast("timestamp").as("timestamp"))

// Apply watermarking
val withWatermark = data
.withWatermark("timestamp", "10 minutes")

// Do some processing...

// Write data to sink
val query = withWatermark
.writeStream
.format("console")
.start()
query.awaitTermination()
```

'flatMapGroupsWithState' and 'mapGroupsWithState' operations, on the other hand, allow you to define a programmable, per-group data management interface. They can be used when you want to maintain arbitrary state while continuously updating it with new information. In other words, it's a way for you to control how your streaming job handles updating state as new data comes in.

For example, you might be tracking the sessions of users on a website:

```
import org.apache.spark.sql.streaming.GroupState
```

```
case class InputRow(userId: String, timestamp: java.sql.Timestamp, eventId:
    Long)
case class UserSession(userId: String, var lastEventId: Long, var
    lastTimestamp: java.sql.Timestamp)

def trackStateFunc(key: String, values: Iterator[InputRow], state: GroupState
    [UserSession]): UserSession = {
  // If this is the first event, create a new UserSession
  if (state.hasTimedOut) {
    val initialSession = UserSession(key, -1, new java.sql.Timestamp(0L))
    state.update(initialSession)
    initialSession
  } else {
    // Update the session
    val existingSession = state.get
    values.foreach { event =>
      if (event.eventId > existingSession.lastEventId && event.timestamp.after
          (existingSession.lastTimestamp)) {
        existingSession.lastEventId = event.eventId
        existingSession.lastTimestamp = event.timestamp
      }
    }
    state.update(existingSession)
    existingSession
  }
}

val result = withWatermark
.groupByKey(_.userId)
.flatMapGroupsWithState(OutputMode.Append, GroupStateTimeout.NoTimeout())(
    trackStateFunc)
```

In this example, for a given 'userId', the 'trackStateFunc' function
updates its corresponding 'UserSession' state based on the incoming
'InputRow's.

6.6 Describe the internal architecture of Spark's Delta Lake. How does it ensure ACID transactions?

Spark's Delta Lake is a high-performance, reliable data lake built on
top of a storage system like HDFS or cloud storage systems such as
S3. It brings ACID transactions to big data workloads, with scalable
metadata handling, data versioning, and unified batch and stream
processing. Let's explore its internal architecture:

The Delta Lake storage layer is a columnar format that includes Parquet for the on-disk storage, combined with a transaction log that tracks changes to the dataset or table.

The internal architecture mainly comprises two components:

1. **Delta Log**: This transaction log is key to Delta Lake's ACID compliance. It is structured as a collection of JSON files stored in a "_delta_log" directory in the root table directory and gets updated with every transaction. When a transaction starts, it reads the Delta Log to ensure it has a consistent snapshot of the data in the Delta Lake table.

2. **Data Files**: These are in Apache Parquet format, a very efficient, column-oriented data storage system with schemes that can be evolved.

Moreover, Delta Lake has an _Optimistic Concurrency Control_ mechanism to handle transactions. When a transaction is ready to commit, it ensures that the data read during the transaction is still the same. If it's unchanged, the transaction's write is committed to the Delta Log.

Here's the basic workflow:

- A table in Delta Lake is a directory containing Parquet files along with a transaction log that records all changes made to the table.

- When a transaction is completed, Delta Lake writes the actions as ordered, atomic commits in JSON format in the Delta Log.

- The state of the table at any point in time can be replicated by replaying the transaction log.

The ACID properties in Delta Lake are enforced as follows:

- **Atomicity**: All changes within a given transaction are treated as a single atomic unit, meaning it either completely succeeds or fails.

- **Consistency**: Delta Lake ensures that any read or write to the table sees a consistent snapshot of the table.

- **Isolation**: Delta Lake optimistically logs a transaction and checks for conflicts with other concurrent transactions before committing. This provides _serializability_, the highest level of isolation.

- **Durability**: Once data is written in Delta, it's safely stored in a storage system with replication.

```
# Sample write operation in Delta Lake

dataframe
  .write
  .format("delta")
  .mode("overwrite")
  .save("/delta/events")
```

This operation will first write out a new set of Parquet files, then update the Delta Log atomically to add these new files. If any part of this operation fails, the entire operation will fail and result in a consistent state in accordance with the ACID principles.

6.7   Explain the intricacies of Spark's dynamic allocation and external shuffle service when used together.

Apache Spark's dynamic resource allocation and external Shuffle Service are powerful features, particularly for managing Spark resources and improving job performance in a multi-tenant environment.

Dynamic Allocation: Dynamic Allocation is a feature in Apache Spark which allows it to add/remove executor resources to an application on the fly depending on the workload. This allows the resources to be allocated when they are needed (during a job) and deallocated when they are not, thereby making the cluster resources usage more efficient.

So, when a Spark job starts, it may start with a few executors, and as the job progresses and the demand for resources increases, new executors are added. When the demand decreases, the extra executors are removed.

Here is how to enable dynamic allocation in the spark configuration:

```
sparkConf.set("spark.dynamicAllocation.enabled", "true")
sparkConf.set("spark.shuffle.service.enabled", "true")
sparkConf.set("spark.dynamicAllocation.initialExecutors", "2")
sparkConf.set("spark.dynamicAllocation.minExecutors", "2")
sparkConf.set("spark.dynamicAllocation.maxExecutors", "10")
```

The above configuration indicates that the Spark job will initially start with 2 executors (initialExecutors) and depending on the workload can scale up to 10 executors (maxExecutors). The job will always have at least 2 executors (minExecutors).

External Shuffle Service: Spark's external shuffle service is a mechanism which allows the executors to be stateless. This facilitates dynamic allocation because a stateless executor can be killed (after its idle timeout) without affecting the progress of ongoing computations.

The external shuffle service creates its own copy of the shuffle data independently of the executors. The shuffle data is stored in an off-heap memory buffer and is served by a separate Netty event loop. This design allows the external shuffle service to handle a high volume of shuffle connections and transfer large amounts of shuffle data with minimal CPU and memory overhead.

External Shuffle Service works in unison with Dynamic Allocation as follows:

- Executors which are idle and have been idle for a certain amount of time (spark.dynamicAllocation.executorIdleTimeout) are candidates for removal.

- However, if these executors hold shuffle data needed by an ongoing or upcoming job, Spark won't be able to remove them, as otherwise doing so would result in the loss of this shuffle data.

- This problem is solved by external shuffle service, which takes ownership of serving the shuffle data from those executors. Once the service takes over, the executors can be safely removed.

To enable the external shuffle service in the Spark configuration:

```
sparkConf.set("spark.shuffle.service.enabled", "true")
```

In conclusion, with dynamic allocation and the external shuffle service, Spark can work more efficiently in a multi-tenant environment
by accurately allocating and deallocating resources based on demand
and without the fear of losing shuffle data.

6.8   How does Spark handle large-scale graph processing, especially with the GraphX library?

Apache Spark is excellent at large-scale graph processing, thanks to
the GraphX library. GraphX is Spark's API for graph computation,
unifying ETL (Extract, Transform, Load), exploratory analysis, and
iterative graph computation into a single system. This means you
can view the same data as graphs and collections, transform and
join graphs with RDDs (Resilient Distributed Dataset) efficiently, and
write custom iterative graph algorithms using the Pregel API.

In more detail, GraphX works by parallelizing data processing across
a distributed infrastructure. Graphs in GraphX are represented by
two collections of properties: vertex properties and edge properties.
Vertex properties hold the properties of each vertex (node) in the
graph. Similarly, edge properties hold the properties of each edge in
the graph.

GraphX provides several core operators for graph computation:

- **Subgraph operator**: It creates a new graph from the existing graph
based on the conditions given on vertices and edges. Conditions on vertices will result in the formation of a new graph with the vertices that
satisfy the given condition.

- **Join operators**: GraphX provides various join operators like joinVertices, join, outerJoinVertices for joining the property graphs with RDDs.

- **Map operators**: It also provides map operators like mapVertices, mapEdges, mapTriplets to transform the properties of the vertices and edges but keep the original graph structure.

- **Aggregate Messages Operator**: It is a flexible communication operator through which users can express more computation than map-reduce operations. It allows the vertices of a graph to communicate with each other by sending messages along the edges.

For example, you can use below Scala code to create a graph in GraphX:

```scala
import org.apache.spark.graphx._

// To make some of the examples work we will also need RDD
import org.apache.spark.rdd.RDD

// Create an RDD for the vertices
val users: RDD[(VertexId, (String, String))] =
  sc.parallelize(Array((3L, ("rxin", "student")), (7L, ("jgonzal", "postdoc"))
  ,
                       (5L, ("franklin", "prof")), (2L, ("istoica", "prof")))))

// Create an RDD for edges
val relationships: RDD[Edge[String]] =
  sc.parallelize(Array(Edge(3L, 7L, "collab"), Edge(5L, 3L, "advisor"),
                       Edge(2L, 5L, "colleague"), Edge(5L, 7L, "pi")))

// Define a default user in case there are relationships with missing user
val defaultUser = ("John Doe", "Missing")

// Build the initial Graph
val graph = Graph(users, relationships, defaultUser)
```

For large-scale graph processing, GraphX can leverage all of Spark's features like in-memory computation, fault tolerance, scalability, and ease of use. You can process graphs with billions of vertices and edges using GraphX, and it enables conducting complex analytics at scale.

Moreover, for algorithms such as PageRank or Connected Components, GraphX includes a set of graph algorithms and builders to simplify graph analytics tasks. The GraphX Pregel API also facilitates the implementation of iterative algorithms.

In conclusion, GraphX combines the advantages of both data-parallel and graph-parallel systems by efficiently expressing graph computation within the Spark computation model.

6.9   Discuss the challenges of integrating Spark with deep learning frameworks. How does Project Hydrogen address these challenges?

Apache Spark is a popular distributed data processing engine that is widely used for Big Data analytics. However, when it comes to integrating Spark with deep learning frameworks, a number of challenges tend to arise.

Challenges Integrating Spark with Deep Learning Frameworks:

1. **Inefficiency**: for deep learning tasks, transferring data between JVM and Python or other deep learning frameworks can cause significant communication overhead.

2. **Inflexibility**: Spark's scheduling policy (which is optimized for data locality) is not ideal for distributed deep learning and other machine learning workloads that require all tasks to run simultaneously.

3. **Unifying abstractions**: Spark's abstractions for data transformation and machine learning algorithms do not natively support deep learning models.

Given these challenges, many big data and AI infrastructure teams have been trying to address these issues. This has led to the creation of Project Hydrogen, one of the most notable new additions in Apache Spark 2.4.

Project Hydrogen:

Project Hydrogen aims to solve the obstacles mentioned above and make it easier and more efficient to utilize Spark with deep learning frameworks.

1. **Barrier execution mode**:

This is a new scheduling mode in Spark that supports tasks that
need to run in parallel, like MPI tasks. This mode enables near-
synchronous processing, which is vital for machine learning and deep
learning workloads.

```
rdd.barrier().mapPartitions(myFunc)
```

2. **Accelerator-aware scheduling**:

Project Hydrogen introduces the ability for Spark to understand and
schedule tasks accounting for the availability of accelerators like GPUs,
which are commonly used in deep learning tasks.

3. **Data interchange protocol**:

A standard API for efficient data interchange has been proposed.
This will avoid serialization and deserialization overhead and high
JVM garbage collection costs when data moves between Spark and
deep learning frameworks.

The combined effect of these additions to Spark is to make deep
learning and machine learning with Spark much more efficient and
scalable, helping it to continue to be a leading platform for Big Data
analytics and AI.

6.10 Dive deep into Spark's code generation mechanism. How does it optimize query execution at runtime?

Apache Spark's code generation mechanism is an integral part of its
query execution engine, which significantly enhances the runtime performance of Spark applications. It eliminates the overhead of inter-

preting complex Spark plans, object creation, and other JVM ineffi-
ciencies. Here I will present a detailed explanation of Spark's code
generation.

When executing your Spark script, Spark will first create a logical
plan, then convert it into a physical plan. At this stage, Spark's
Catalyst optimizer plays a vital role in optimizing this physical plan,
which is when code generation happens. Spark's code generation
refers to the process of generating Java bytecode at runtime that can
implement the operations described in the physical plan.

Following is the step-by-step process outlining the Spark's Whole-
Stage Code Generation (a key mechanism for query optimization):

1) Logical Plan: Once a Dataframe/Dataset/SQL operation is
invoked, Spark creates a logical plan.

2) Physical Plan: Spark's Catalyst Optimizer transforms this logical plan into a series of physical execution plans.

3) Whole-Stage Code Generation: In this step, multiple physical
operations are fused together into a single Java function, which we
call a "Whole-stage CodeGen". It significantly decreases the CPU
execution time by compressing many operations into a single function,
removing virtual function calls, and allowing the JIT compiler of the
JVM to optimize the code better.

The name "Whole-Stage" comes from this diagram of a query plan:

```
[Input] -> [Filter] -> [Aggregate] -> [Output]
```

A "stage" in this context is a contiguous series of operations that can
be collapsed into a single function.

Here is a code representation of these steps:

```
val df = spark.range(10) // Logical Plan
val df2 = df.filter("id > 1") // Still Logical Plan
df2.count() // Trigger the Physical Plan, Whole-stage CodeGen
```

Use 'df2.explain(true)' to get detailed information on the Logical
Plan, Optimized Logical Plan, Physical Plan and Whole-stage Code-
Gen.

In summary, Spark's code generation optimizes your Spark queries
by reducing the function call overhead, enabling loop unrolling, and
other JVM JIT compiler optimizations. It is one of the reasons why
Spark SQL can be much faster than RDD operations. Whole-Stage
Code generation optimizes Spark SQL's physical execution plan by
collapsing it into a single function, eliminating virtual function calls,
and enabling more aggressive compiler optimization from the JVM's
JIT compiler.

6.11 How does Spark handle data skewness during joins, and what are the internal optimizations?

Apache Spark handles data skewness during joins by using 2 internal optimizations: Adaptive Query Execution (AQE) and Avoiding
Exchange Reuse.

1. Adaptive Query Execution (AQE): Starting from Spark 3.0, AQE
re-optimizes and adjusts the query plan based on the runtime statistics. It dynamically handles skew join instead of pre-splitting the
skewed keys before join. For example, suppose we have two datasets
with keys A and B. If key A is extremely skewed, during execution
if AQE sees that too many rows for A are going to one task, it will
re-optimize the plan to add splits for A.

For enabling AQE, you need to set the following configuration:

```
spark.conf.set("spark.sql.adaptive.enabled", "true")
```

2. Avoiding Exchange Reuse: By avoiding the data shuffling operation, which can be very expensive, Spark can optimize the execution

of jobs. But in situations where there is skew in keys, this optimization can be turned off to handle the situation. By doing this,
Spark avoids using a single partition for skewed keys and distributes
it among multiple partitions.

We can avoid reuse of Exchange by setting the following configuration
to false.

```
spark.conf.set("spark.sql.exchange.reuse", "false")
```

But remember, these configurations should be used judiciously because avoiding exchange reuse means more data shuffling - which can
lead to more network I/O and the overhead of materializing the shuffle operations. AQE is generally safe to use in most of the cases as it
adapts based on runtime statistics.

Note: Skew Join in Apache Spark is an advanced topic, understanding
it fully takes a bit of time and experience with tuning Spark jobs.
Need to be careful while setting these optimizations as they can have
larger impact on your Spark job's performance.

6.12   Discuss the internal workings of Spark's Continuous Processing mode in Structured Streaming.

Continuous Processing mode in Spark Structured Streaming provides
end-to-end latencies as low as 1 ms with at-least-once fault-tolerance
guarantees. This is an experimental feature introduced from Spark
2.3.0 and it targets use cases where low-latency requirements are
paramount.

With Continuous Processing mode, the stream is treated as an infinite
table where new rows are appended to the input table. In other words,
it's as if we are running the query continuously on the changing input
data. Here's a diagram of how the stream processing works:

```
Input Table (Stream) ---> Query ---> Result Table
```

The input table is the stream of input data. The query sees this as
a table on which computations (like aggregation, filtering, or window
functions) can be performed. The result of the query is a new table
that is generated incrementally as new input data arrives. This table
is essentially the processed stream of data.

Unlike the micro-batch mode in Structured Streaming which processes data in small batches, Continuous Processing mode processes
data record by record, providing millisecond-level latency.

The Continuous Processing mode uses the ContinuousExecution class
which keeps track of the offsets that are being processed within each
spark job, it's similar to the epoch id in the micro-batch mode but
rather than batching a group of records, it's pulling one single record
at a time.

Each node that is running the query concurrently will continue to
pull from the source, processing the records as they come in, pushing
them downstream afterward. Fault tolerance works by tracking the
processed offsets within the job's metadata.

Continuous Processing works great for certain workloads, such as
read-time operations, scoring, and machine learning. However, it's
important to note that it is still in an experimental stage.

Here is what it would look like in code:

```
val input_df = spark.readStream.format("kafka")
.option("kafka.bootstrap.servers", "localhost:9092")
.option("subscribe", "sample_topic")
.load()

val output_df = input_df.selectExpr("CAST(key AS STRING)", "CAST(value AS
    STRING)")

val query = output_df.writeStream
.trigger(Trigger.Continuous("1 second")) // calls the continuous processing
.outputMode("append")
.format("console")
.start()
```

In this case, the query will be triggered for processing every 1 second.

Please note that the above level of code is an abstracted simplification of what is happening under the hood. There are many complex and well-optimized mechanics at play to support Spark's continuous processing mode.

6.13 How does Spark manage and optimize broadcast joins for extremely large datasets?

Broadcast joins in Spark are useful when you have a large dataset and a small dataset that fit comfortably in memory. Here, the small dataset is broadcasted to all the task nodes where the large dataset partitions reside. Now, all the data needed to perform the join is local to the task. This avoids the high cost of data shuffling which is a common problem in spark's shuffle join.

However, when it comes to extremely large datasets, managing and optimizing broadcast joins could be tricky because by default, Spark will try to broadcast every common join across the data, which can cause memory errors if your data is too large.

Here are a few ways to manage and optimize broadcast joins for large datasets:

1. Increase Driver Memory and Executor Memory:

By increasing the driver memory and executor memory, you can allow larger datasets to be broadcasted. However, this method has a limitation as broadcasting extremely large datasets can still cause Out-of-Memory (OOM) errors. For example,

```
spark-submit --driver-memory 20g --executor-memory 50g
```

2. Manually Broadcasting Large Tables:

You can manually control broadcast joins by using the broadcast hint 'broadcast()' in your Spark SQL queries or DataFrame API. This function tells Spark that the DataFrame involved will be small enough to fit into memory and should be broadcasted. Example:

```
from pyspark.sql.functions import broadcast
largeDF.join(broadcast(smallDF), "id")
```

3. Using 'autoBroadcastJoinThreshold':

You can use 'spark.sql.autoBroadcastJoinThreshold' configuration property to control the maximum size of the dataset (in bytes) to be broadcasted. By setting this value as -1, broadcasting is turned off; and by setting the value to a higher number, you are allowing larger datasets to be broadcasted. However, be careful not to set this value too high as it may cause OOM errors. You need to find the right balance.

```
spark.conf.set("spark.sql.autoBroadcastJoinThreshold", 100 * 1024 * 1024)
```

4. Using Broadcast Variables:

Broadcast variables allow the programmer to keep a read-only variable cached on each machine instead of sending a copy of it with tasks. They can be used to give every node a copy of a large input dataset in an efficient manner.

```
broadcastVar = sc.broadcast([1, 2, 3])
v = broadcastVar.value
```

Remember, using broadcast joins is generally more efficient if the broadcasted DataFrame can fit into memory, as it minimizes the expensive operations like network I/O, data serialization, and shuffling. However, you need to be careful with the memory settings and configurations to avoid potential OOM errors.

6.14 Describe the intricacies of checkpointing in Spark Streaming, especially in high-concurrency scenarios.

Checkpointing in Spark Streaming is a mechanism that saves the state of a streaming application at certain intervals of time to enable recovery from failures. It plays two important roles:

1. Fault Tolerance:checkpointing recovers lost data and metadata due to worker or driver failures, ensuring the reliability of the data processing.

2. Achieving exactly-once semantics: Some of the operations within Spark streaming also need checkpointing to guarantee that the data is processed exactly once even under failures.

Now in high-concurrency scenarios, multiple concurrent jobs will write to the checkpoint directory.

This can be a taxing process and might slow down Spark Streaming. The most critical point to understand in such scenarios is that while Spark Streaming does support concurrent checkpointing, the support comes with an important caveat.

To handle high-concurrency scenarios effectively, consider the following important elements:

1. Checkpoint Directory: This should ideally be a replicated file system like HDFS. It ensures even in case where a node running Spark Streaming goes down, the application can still recover using checkpoints from other alive nodes.

```
ssc.checkpoint("hdfs://localhost:9000/checkpoint")
```

2. Window / Slice Duration: The batch interval or window duration should be effectively decided to optimize recovery speed and storage overhead. Shorter intervals would require more frequent updates,

leading to a slower recovery process in comparison to longer durations.

3. Finalizing checkpoint files: Since checkpoint files are append-only, delays may arise while finalizing them. To resolve this, finalize the current checkpoint operation before starting a new one.

4. Deciding what operations need to be checkpointed: Not every operation in Apache Spark needs to be checkpointed. Generally, output operations and those which perist RDDs need to be checkpointed. Be intentional about what gets checkpointed to improve performance.

Remember, efficient handling of checkpointing can add a bit of an overhead to the system, but striking a balance between fault-tolerance and performance is key to managing high-concurrency scenarios effectively in Spark Streaming.

6.15 How does Spark's "barrier execution mode" work, especially for distributed deep learning tasks?

Barrier Execution Mode is a scheduling mode in Apache Spark to facilitate the integration of deep learning and machine learning libraries. Traditionally, distributed deep learning and machine learning workloads require all tasks to complete simultaneously, which is difficult due to variations in execution speed among different tasks in Spark. Barrier Execution Mode intends to handle this issue.

When Barrier Execution Mode is used, each stage of tasks must start simultaneously and CANNOT start until all tasks in the previous stage finish. In other words, all tasks within the same barrier stage depend on each other, so they start and finish at the same time. If any task fails, the entire stage is aborted. This ensures that all tasks in a stage are perfectly aligned in time, thus, satisfying the synchronous update requirements of distributed deep learning tasks.

Here is a fragment of code which illustrates Barrier Execution Mode in Spark:

```
rdd.barrier().mapPartitions(lambda partition: train_deep_learning_model(
    partition)).collect()
```

In the above line, 'rdd.barrier()' sets the RDD into the barrier stage. Then, for each partition of the RDD, we apply the 'train_deep_learning_model' function.

Moreover, the Barrier Execution Mode in Spark also offers the BarrierTaskContext API to allow the tasks to communicate with each other. BarrierTaskContext provides two primary functions:

1. 'allGather()': Each task can collect data from all the other tasks in the form of an array.

2. 'getLocalProperties()': Returns properties set by the driver on a per-task basis.

Relation to distributed deep learning tasks: Distributed deep learning tasks often require all tasks to have the same view of the model and update the parameters synchronously. This is a requirement to ensure that the model learns accurately from the data. Barrier Execution Mode in Apache Spark ensures that all tasks start and finish at the same time (to have the same view of the model) and facilitates synchronous parameter updates across all tasks.

6.16   Discuss the challenges of running Spark on disaggregated storage and compute clusters.

Running Spark on disaggregated storage and compute clusters poses a number of challenges:

1. **Data Shuffling Over Network**: If data and computation are lo-

cated in separate systems, data required for computation needs to be moved from the storage system to the compute cluster. This so-called 'data shuffling' can add significant overhead and network latency, especially in large-scale systems.

2. **I/O Bottlenecks**: Disaggregated storage and compute clusters often suffer from I/O bottlenecks due to the significant amount of data that needs to be transferred between the two systems. This problem becomes even more pronounced when dealing with large-scale data processing tasks.

3. **Data Locality**: The principle of data locality is compromised. Data locality, where computation is moved to the location of the data, is a key advantage in traditional Hadoop MapReduce tasks. By separating storage and compute, operations incur significant network I/O costs as data has to be moved to the compute nodes.

4. **Consistency Issues**: When storage and compute are separated, it may lead to consistency issues. For instance, Spark computations may not reflect the most recent state of the data in the storage systems if any changes are made to the data during computation.

5. **Resource Management**: Managing resources can be difficult in a disaggregated environment. The system must be able to handle spikes in demand for compute or storage resources, while also making sure that resources are not sitting idle. For Spark, this also means it has to rely on an external system like Mesos or YARN for managing resources across the two systems.

To overcome these challenges, organizations can employ a few strategies:

- Using high-speed networks to reduce the latency added by network transmission.

- Making use of data partitioning and bucketing techniques to reduce cross-network data shuffles.

- Utilizing in-memory data structures to minimize the impact of I/O operations.

- Implementing strong consistency models in the storage systems.

- Efficient resource scheduling and capacity planning.

Here is a simple example of how data partitioning in Spark can help reduce network shuffles:

```
val inputRDD = sparkContext.textFile("path/to/data")
val partitionedRDD = inputRDD.partitionBy(new HashPartitioner(100))
```

Overall, while disaggregate storage and computation offers flexibility and individual scaling, it can introduce latency and management overhead. Careful engineering and resource management strategies are required to mitigate these issues when running Spark on disaggregated storage and compute clusters.

6.17 How does Spark handle nested data structures and optimizations for the same?

Apache Spark has a powerful feature to support complex data types and nested data structures including array, map, and struct in RDD, DataFrame and Dataset. This feature helps you in loading, processing and analysis of complex and nested data more easily.

Here's a brief explanation of how it handles nested data structures in DataFrame.

Let's say we have a JSON data as follows:

```
{
  "id": "123",
  "name": "John",
  "addresses": [
    {
      "city": "New York",
      "state": "NY"
    },
    {
      "city": "Los Angeles",
      "state": "CA"
```

```
    },
    ...
  ]
}
```

And we want to read this data into a DataFrame. The schema of the DataFrame will look like this:

```
root
 |-- id: string (nullable = true)
 |-- name: string (nullable = true)
 |-- addresses: array (nullable = true)
 |    |-- element: struct (containsNull = true)
 |    |    |-- city: string (nullable = true)
 |    |    |-- state: string (nullable = true)
```

To access fields in the nested data, we can use the dot (.) operator combined with the field name. For instance, to access the city of the first address, we can use 'addresses[0].city'.

Optimizations for Nested Data:

Regarding optimizations, Spark uses various techniques such as predicate pushdown and projection pushdown to optimize the processing of nested data.

- Predicate pushdown: Spark pushes filter predicates into the data source to reduce the amount of data read. If there are filters on the nested fields, Spark can push these filters at the time of reading, which reduces the amount of data read and hence improves the performance.

- Projection pushdown: Similar to predicate pushdown, projection pushdown is about selecting only the necessary fields. Spark can push the schema required for the final result down to the data source, so unnecessary columns can be discarded at an early stage.

For instance, if we only need the name and the cities of the addresses, we could write 'df.select("name", "addresses.city")', and Spark will only read the necessary fields, which can significantly reduce the data size and increase query speed. However, keep in mind that these optimizations may not work for all the data sources or file formats.

Lastly, Apache Spark has an optimization feature called 'spark.sql. optimizer.nestedSchemaPruning.enabled', when enabled, optimizes reading nested fields from file formats that can prune nested schemas, such as Parquet, ORC etc. This is used to reduce I/O and alleviates the costs of reading unneeded nested columns. This optimization is disabled by default and can be enabled by setting 'spark.sql.optimizer. nestedSchemaPruning.enabled' to 'true'.

6.18   Dive deep into Spark's UDF (User Defined Function) optimizations, especially with Python UDFs.

Apache Spark UDF, which stands for User-Defined Function, is a feature of Spark SQL to define new functions for DataFrame or SQL datasets and incorporate them into Spark's SQL Catalyst Optimizer. It is considerably efficient with Scala UDFs as they run on the JVM.

However, native Python UDFs have some limitations. Spark UDFs written in Python run in Python interpreter and use Py4J to interact with the JVM, causing high performance overhead due to serialization and invocation costs.

Let's consider an example of a Python UDF:

```
from pyspark.sql.functions import udf
from pyspark.sql.types import IntegerType

def square(x):
  return x**2

spark.udf.register("squareFunction", square, IntegerType())

df = spark.createDataFrame([(1,),(2,),(3,)], ['value'])
df.withColumn('squared_value', udf_square('value')).show()
```

The 'square' is Python UDF which takes a number and returns the square. While this works, it has considerable performance overhead when you handle big data, as the data needs to go through serialization to be transferred to Python interpreter and then the result has to go through deserialization to be transferred back to JVM.

To address this performance issue, 'Pandas UDFs' and 'Vectorized UDFs' are introduced in Spark 2.3 which leverage Arrow to eliminate the serialization cost, when used with Apache Arrow enabled ('spark.sql.execution.arrow.enabled'=true). They are executed in Arrow's dataframe and therefore much faster than regular Python UDFs.

A similar UDF using Pandas would look like:

```
from pyspark.sql.functions import pandas_udf, PandasUDFType

def square_pandas(x):
  return x**2

square_udf = pandas_udf(square_pandas, returnType=IntegerType())
df.withColumn('squared_value', square_udf('value')).show()
```

Here the 'square_pandas' function is a Pandas function which operates on a series of data.

Spark 3.0 introduces a novel extension of Pandas UDFs, called 'Pandas Function APIs' perceived to handle different types of Python functions returning either Series or DataFrame.

```
from pyspark.sql.pandas.functions import pandas_udf

@pandas_udf('integer')
def square_s_pandas(s: pd.Series) -> pd.Series:
   return s ** 2

df.select(square_s_pandas(df.value)).show()
```

Using these UDF optimizations, you can achieve better performance and scalability in Spark and also combine the power of Python with Spark.

6.19   Explain the internal architecture and challenges of Spark's push-based shuffle service.

Spark has an existing shuffle system known as Sort-Merge Join, but this process doesn't fully utilize the available memory and CPU. Having recognized this issue, the Spark community developed a new Push-based shuffle feature starting from version 3.1.0.

Push-based shuffle has two stages, as opposed to the traditional one reduce stage. The two stages are the map and merge stages.

In the map stage, all the mapper tasks finish and generate shuffle partition files, just like in ordinary shuffle. But here, the difference is, the mapper tasks will also generate index files. So the mapper tasks not only produce data, but at the same time, they will also provide the location of their data.

In the merge stage, a specified number of reduce tasks will be launched to fetch the index files previously generated by the mappers. Once they get the index files, they will identify the shuffle partition files that need to be merged. After these two steps, data merging will happen, leveraging both memory and disks.

These two stages have their executors which will be cached, and because the shuffle partition files are sorted, all the operations are performed in a very efficient manner.

The challenges associated with Spark's push-based shuffle service are:

1. Extra CPU and IO consumption:

Push-based shuffle includes an additional merge procedure, which would increase the burden on the CPU and I/O. In resource-intensive environments, this overhead could lead to bottlenecks restricting the performance.

2. Handling large shuffle blocks:

A shuffle block may be too large to fit into the memory allocated for the shuffle process, causing out-of-memory problems. This issue can be mitigated either by increasing the overall memory allocated to Spark or by reducing the size of each shuffle block.

3. Data skew:

When a particular partition is significantly larger than the others, it could lead to a bottleneck in processing and reduce the overall performance.

4. Potential data loss:

When mapper tasks get preempted by other high priority tasks before they finish or if they fail midway, the corresponding index files and shuffle data can be lost, leading to potential data loss.

5. Network stability:

The file-based shuffle service depends heavily on network connectivity and performance. Network fluctuations or low performance can seriously impact the shuffle procedure.

In summary, while Spark's push-based shuffle service offers improved performance over its sort-merge shuffle, it still requires careful management to ensure its optimal performance.

6.20   Discuss the intricacies and challenges of integrating Spark with emerging data storage formats and systems.

Apache Spark is a robust big data processing engine that provides scalable and efficient data processing and analytics services. It supports a number of storage systems, making it a go-to solution for or-

ganizations that handle big data. However, while integrating Spark
with emerging data storage formats and systems, there can be several
challenges and intricacies.

1. File Formats: Spark supports various file formats such as Parquet, Avro, CSV, JSON, etc, as well as data from HDFS, S3, and
HBase. However, not all file formats provide the same benefits. For
instance, CSV and JSON are easy to use but lack the support for
schema evolution and compression. On the contrary, Parquet and
Avro are more performant and provide support for schema evolution
and compression, but they're binary formats and hence, difficult to
debug.

2. Non-Relational Data Store Support: While Spark connects to
various data sources, it provides limited support for non-relational
data store systems, like MongoDB, Cassandra, DynamoDB, etc. It
can handle these non-relational databases using custom Spark con-
nectors, but this requires additional configurations and can be a bit
challenging to setup. For instance, integrating Spark with Cassandra
requires the Spark-Cassandra connector:

```
./bin/spark-shell --packages com.datastax.spark:spark-cassandra-connector_2
    .11:2.4.0 --conf spark.cassandra.connection.host=127.0.0.1
```

3. Maintainability: Integrating Spark with different storage systems
can be high maintenance, as each storage system can have different
CRUD operations, and schema definition and evolution. It requires
a close monitoring for potential errors and latency issues.

4. Data Consistency: Ensuring data consistency is a major challenge
when handling data from multiple sources. Not all storage system
provides strong consistency, and as a result, data can vary between
reads, leading to possible issues with data quality.

5. Prioritizing Speed and Scale: When integrating Spark with a new
data storage format or system, a critical aspect to consider is how
well the storage system scales and how fast it can process and retrieve
data. Some systems may prioritize speed while others may emphasize
scale. For large scale data processing, it's essential to find a balance

between these two that fits your specific use case.

6. Dependency Management: Different storage systems might need different versions of the same dependency. This might create a conflict and can be a challenge to manage.

Despite these challenges, integrating Spark with various storage systems offers a lot of flexibility and scalability, making it a preferred choice for big data analysis and processing.